Captain for Life

Captain for Life

and other temporary assignments

John Harkes
with Denise Kiernan

SLEEPING BEAR PRESS

Library of Congress Cataloging-in-Publication Data

Harkes, John.
     Captain for life : and other temporary assignments / by John
 Harkes with Denise Kiernan.
          p.   cm.
     ISBN 1-886947-49-X
     1. Harkes, John. 2. Soccer players—United States—Biography.
     I. Kiernan, Denise.   II. Title.
     GV942.7.H336A3   1999
     796.334'092—dc21
     [B] ·   98-49649
                                                      CIP

Sleeping Bear Press
121 South Main
P.O. Box 20
Chelsea, MI 48118
www.sleepingbearpress.com

Printed and bound in Canada.

10 9 8 7 6 5 4 3 2 1

Acknowledgments

In this day and age of professional sports, it is so easy to get caught up in all the hype, concentrating solely on money and notoriety and losing sight of what it's all about. After 27 years, I still enjoy being a soccer player.

I measure success by the quality of the people around me, not by materialistic things. I have been fortunate to have more than my share of amazing friends, family, and other supporters who have believed in me and stuck with me through thick and thin. Neither my career nor this book would exist without them.

In particular, I would like to thank my wife, Cindi, and my two children, Ian and Lauren, for their support, understanding, and patience not only during the writing of this book, but all the time. Being a husband and father is the most important and cherished "assignment" I will ever have. Special thanks must go to my parents, Jimmy and Jessie. I wouldn't be here without their hard work, love, and sacrifice. My dad was my first coach and he remains my greatest influence. I'd also like to thank my extended family, especially Cindi's parents, Ron and Sue Kunihiro, for their help and support over the years.

I'm grateful for the incredible friends who have always been there and kept me laughing, and continue to remind me that it's only a game of football. (E-zay, the boys!) And I'm lucky to have played with and for any number of outstanding teammates and coaches at every level. There are far too many to list. I also want to thank my agent, Craig Sharon, not only for his help and guidance with my career and this book, but also for his friendship. And his wife, Christina, must also be thanked for her patience, hospitality, and understanding. I'd also like to thank my writing partner, Denise Kiernan, for spending many hours listening to my story and organizing my chaotic life. I know this seemed like a daunting task and I truly appreciate her perseverance and hard work.

And finally, I'd like to thank my fans, especially all the kids, for their years of loyal support, encouragement, and belief in me as a person, player, and role model. It means a world of difference to an athlete and it has meant everything to me.

—J. H.

I would like to thank all the friends, family, players, coaches, and colleagues who contributed their time, energy, and memories to this project, especially my agent, Jon Rosen, David Davis, Jeff Klein, Alexi Lalas, and George Vecsey. I'd like to thank Mel and Marilyn Stein and Chris and Lorna Waddle for taking care of me while I was on the other side of the pond. And I'd especially like to thank Craig and Christina Sharon for their incredible hospitality, and my family and friends for their support and understanding. And finally, thank you to John and Cindi Harkes for their willingness to openly share the experiences of their lives, good and bad, with me.

—D. K.

Foreword

Captain for Life and Other Temporary Assignments is a truly interesting book about the soccer career of John Harkes. I have known John and his family for approximately 15 years, and I feel honored to comment on John and this chronicled celebration of his career.

My first recollection of John was in his "wee man" days at Kearny High School. I witnessed Kearny's state championship game in his freshman year. It was pretty obvious that John was a special player and had a bright future, if he could position himself to make the big step of leaving Kearny to pursue an education and/or career in soccer. The rest, of course, is history, and as we look back on his career, one can say that his accomplishments may not be matched by another American for many years to come. We must remember that John's résumé in soccer includes the following:

- High School All-American
- National High School Player of the Year
- College All-American
- National Collegiate Player of the Year
- 1988 U.S. Olympic Team Member
- Eleven Years, U.S. National Team Member
- 90 Caps
- Captain of the Kearny High School, University of Virginia, D.C. United, and U.S. National Teams
- Participant, Two World Cups
- Co-MVP 1995 Copa America
- 1996 World All Star
- Winner, England Goal of the Year
- League Cup Winner's Medal

- F.A. Cup Final Player
- U.S. Open Cup Championship Winner
- CONCACAF Champions Cup Winner
- Two-time MLS Cup Championship Winner
- InterAmerican Cup Championship Winner

I think you get the point. John Harkes is the most accomplished player in the history of U.S. soccer. I am certainly proud to have been a part of John's career as his coach at both the University of Virginia and D.C. United.

On a personal level, I have witnessed John's growth in a very challenging academic and social environment at the University of Virginia, which was quite a change from the streets of Kearny, New Jersey! I have seen John play at Wembley, play in two World Cup series, hold the MLS Cup above his head, marry his college girlfriend (Cindi Kunihiro), experience the thrill of becoming a father for the first time (the birth of Ian), christen his daughter (Lauren), and experience the disappointment of not being a part of the 1998 U.S. World Cup team in France. Both John and Cindi have been wonderful friends to my wife, Phyllis, and have been very supportive to my son, Kenny. Needless to say, John and his family have played an important role in the lives of the Arena family.

Admittedly, our soccer relationship has not always been the smoothest ride for either one of us. We have had our disagreements and tense moments. We have also experienced the enjoyment and rewards stemming from successful teams. Overall, I think we can both say it's been a good relationship for two rather stubborn and competitive individuals. We have both survived and I think we are better people for having experienced the relationship. I can only hope that our friendship continues well past soccer.

Captain for Life and Other Temporary Assignments is great reading for players and coaches. Rarely has the U.S. soccer community had the opportunity to follow the career of one of our own. *Captain for Life* is the inside story about an American player who has played a key role in soccer at its highest level. For players, it shows the enormous pressure placed on professionals, both on and off the field of play. For coaches, it offers a perspective of the issues you need to deal with on a daily basis if you wish to be successful. It shows that we are all vulnerable to tough decisions in our lives— sometimes fair and sometimes unfair. The lives of professional athletes and coaches are short-term, and we can never let our guards down.

Enjoy the book and keep in mind that the last chapter has yet to be written. I'm hopeful that when all is said and done, John can feel good about what he's accomplished in the sport of soccer—he should!

Bruce Arena

Contents

1 | The Yank Has Arrived

"**W**hat are you on about, Yankee boy? Too cold for ya, is it?"

Well it was, actually. December in England is not exactly short-sleeve weather. Not for me, anyway. It was more dreary than usual and not the kind of setting that made me think I'd be having one of the most important nights of my life. I was boarding the bus with the rest of the Sheffield Wednesday players; we had drawn Derby County in a League Cup match and I was on the way to what I hoped would be my third match as a starter with Wednesday. The League Cup is played every year in England. There are tournament games throughout the regular club season with the finals in the spring, and the competition is open to teams in all divisions. This game was important and I hadn't been playing with the club for very long, so I tried not to get my hopes up about being in the starting eleven.

The bus ride from Sheffield to Derby took about an hour. I sat there, looking around at everyone, very nervous. I'd never been to a League Cup match, so I had no idea what to expect. And I'd only been in Sheffield for a few months and was still getting to know the other players. At the same time, they were trying to decide what to make of me, and I felt a bit out of place. It was December 12, 1990, Christmas was coming, and I knew there was no way I'd be able to make it back to the States. During the ride to Derby, I was listening to John Sheridan, "Shez," our playmaker, talk about the Derby squad. He was telling me who to watch out for, and explaining how important this match was and what the Cup would mean to the club. Sheffield Wednesday was hoping to advance to England's top division the following year and a lot was riding on every game. I just wanted the chance to get out on the field, and I certainly had no idea what a difference one game could make.

Each game was still an adjustment for me, and the players said this one would be even more intense: the atmosphere, the fans singing and chanting in the stands, and the Derby players hammering you to bits on the field. One of the great things about England, though, is that you have traveling supporters. Two or three thousand fans travel with you and go to bat for you in the crowd, separated, hopefully, from the home supporters. The surroundings and the competition at that level—the fast play and the rough tackles—were a huge thrill for me.

It was freezing cold that night—the air damp from flurries that stopped just before the game—and the pitch was really hard. We started out warming up in our sweats, but most of the guys soon took those off. It was part of the hard-nosed, no nonsense "be a man about it" attitude that was so common over there. When everybody's sweats came off, I looked around and noticed that Shez, Phil King, and most of the other veteran players had long-sleeve jerseys on. I, on the other hand, was wearing short sleeves, and I couldn't remember what my forearms felt like. When we finished warming up, I decided to have a cup of tea to keep warm. I walked over to have a chat with the trainer. Alan Smith was his name, but we called him "Smudge-O." He was full of life, about 45 years old, and probably the fittest guy out there. I quietly said, "Hey, Smudge-O, I noticed that some of the guys are wearing long-sleeve jerseys. I was wondering if I could get ahold of one of those myself."

Big mistake.

Smudge-O looked at me like I'd asked him for a pair of silk long underwear and howled, "Long-sleeve shirt?! Whadya mean *long-sleeve* shirt?!" His voice kept getting louder and louder and then he started looking around at the other players to get them to start winding me up, too. That didn't take long. "What ya need a long-sleeve shirt for? Get out and play, ya Yank." By then our manager, Ron Atkinson, had heard enough and he turned around and chimed in, "Who's that, then? Yankee boy—what are you yelling about son, *long-sleeve* shirt?" So I started backpedaling, stammering, and trying to explain, "Uh, well, I was just wondering . . . I see some players wearing, and . . . " He just barked back at me, "Naahhh . . . Ya got your tee-shirt on underneath, get out there!"

So I dropped it, saying, "All right, Gaffer, no problem. I'm cool with that." Which was mistake number two, because then all the other players started mocking me in an American accent, saying, "Hey, man, I'm cool. Are you cool, man? Harkesy says he's cool . . . " I realized there was no way I could win, so I shut up altogether. Then Atkinson called me over and I thought to myself, "Great, he's not done with me yet." But instead, he told me that I was starting. I was starting in a League Cup match, at right back. He said, "You're doing well for us, Harkesy, son. Keep it going; same thing again. You know how to do this." And as I started to head out onto the field, he stopped me.

"Harkesy, before you go out . . . ," he said in a low voice, and handed me a cup. "What's this?" I asked. And Atkinson, not missing a beat, said with a wink, "A shot of brandy, son; that'll warm you up." I thought he had to be kidding. Two minutes before I walk out onto the field to play a League Cup match and my manager was handing me a shot. "No, no, really. Thanks, but no."

"Just get it down your neck and don't worry about it," he said. Well, I respected the hell out of this guy, arguing didn't seem to be an option, and I was cold and nervous. Every match I played I was under a microscope, everyone watching to see if I could handle it. Atkinson knew this. Maybe he was trying to distract me, or maybe just relax me. I don't know. But I downed it. I could feel the brandy going through me and it made me shiver as I thought to myself, "What am I doing? I'm about to go out and play a game." Funny enough, after the shot and all the winding up, I was given a long-sleeve jersey.

The game was your typical local rivalry—brutal, physical, and fast-paced. I was hoping to make it through in one piece. Since it was a Cup game, both teams were going at each other hard, the pace never let up, and there wasn't a lot of possession by either side. But late in the first half things started to turn our way. Little did I realize that one of the most important moments of my career was about to happen.

The ball came out to our left back, Phil King, and Kingy passed it forward 15 yards to Nigel Worthington. Worthington squared the ball to Sheridan who knocked it back to Worthington again. It was the first time we had put more than three passes together, and we were just outside their half. Nigel switched a long ball over to me just as I was coming toward the midfield line; although I was at right back, I was pushing forward. I took the ball on the bounce—like a half-volley—and I pushed up even farther. After another touch I was over the midfield line. I was on the run, about 35 yards out, and something came over me—a feeling, adrenaline, something—and I whacked that ball. I put my head down, planted my left foot, swung my arms up and, at that one moment, my form—everything—was perfect. The ball took off like a rocket, crossing the goal-mouth from right to left, and it sailed into the top left corner, still picking up pace as it hit the net. In goal for Derby County at that time was Peter Shilton, keeper for the English National Team and one of the most-capped and highly respected players of all time. He stretched, but it blew right by him.

David Hirst, one of our strikers, was standing right in front of the goal as the ball went in. It hit the net and post in the back corner, and then bounced out. Hirsty followed it up and kicked in the rebound, just in case the ref thought the ball didn't go in. But by that time I was already on my celebration run, bolting toward the Sheffield fans at the other end of the field, seated behind our goal. Until they saw me running, they couldn't tell whether or not the ball had gone in. But once I took off, the crowd went nuts and people started jumping out of their seats. They were screaming, chanting, climbing on top of each other. The emotion in the stadium was overwhelming, especially for me, because I'd never experienced anything like that before in the States. I ran down the side of the field, pumping my fist, and Sheridan started chasing after me, screaming, "Come 'ere, come 'ere, ya Yankee bastard!"

It was one of the nicest things anyone's ever yelled at me.

I didn't even know where I was going—I'm lucky I didn't end up in the parking lot—and our blue-and-white corner of supporters was bobbing up and down, waving their scarves, and screaming my name. I came back toward the center of the field and Nigel Pearson was standing there staring at me, not believing what I'd just done. Then all of a sudden he broke out in a smile and head-butted me. I started looking around, completely delirious, and I saw Atkinson on the sidelines motioning for me to settle down, which was a pretty tall order at the moment. I was in a new league, trying to stay alive, and I'd just scored one of the best goals of my life. But I knew he was right: I had to focus. We all had to. I thought, "I've got to pull it together. Don't make a mistake, John. Whatever you do, just don't make a mistake now." We were, after all, only 32 minutes into the match, with a long, cold 58 minutes left to go.

Halftime came around and we were still up 1–0. I remember the speech Atkinson gave before we went back out and the way that he talked about my goal. All he said was, "Great goal from Harkesy, brilliant strike from the young lad. But hey—let's not ruin it for the boy, huh? Let's fight, let's win the game." That was it, he didn't harp on it. I respected Atkinson so much, and I still do. The way he talked about me, by not making a big deal out of it, made me feel like I was finally part of the team. He kept things in perspective for me—it was just one goal, after all—but he also acted like he wasn't that surprised by what I'd done. It was as though he knew I had it in me all along. I'm glad someone did. And right then I thought to myself, "Wow—I love this guy." Obviously, I hadn't completely gotten hold of myself yet.

I had gotten so caught up in what he was saying that when we went back out for the second half, I'd already forgotten about the goal, if you can believe that. Derby was putting a lot of pressure on us, and a lot of the play was taking place at our end of the field. They were knocking some great long balls and had the run of the game. I was trying to concentrate on clearing the ball, making sure that I was always on the right angle and that my position was just so. No mistakes, always alert—because they run at you fast in England!

I was on the near post for one of the Derby corners and the ball swung out to the 18. Someone struck a great volley and it went right underneath our goalkeeper. I stretched on the inside and managed to get my toe on it, but it still went in. The game was tied and I was thinking, "No way. We can't lose this game. We can't even *tie* this game. We have to win." We held it together and started to build up some momentum of our own. We were fighting hard and started to get the better of the play. The tables were starting to turn and the pressure was back on Derby, but the minutes were ticking away.

Danny Wilson, who was playing right midfield in front of me at the time, played the ball back to me and I sent it right back to him and started to make an overlapping run. I saw him look up at me and I thought he was going to cross the ball, but he didn't. Instead, he nailed it down the wing to me, and it had a little bit too much pace on it, so I started sprinting. I saw a Derby player out of the corner of my eye coming in fast to challenge me, and I was heading out of bounds and out of play. I barely got to the ball in time, but I whipped it in to the near post, right around the Derby player who slid in hard underneath me. I hit the dirt. But playing up front for us at the time was Paul Williams, a player who always made the right runs. This one was to the near post and, without even thinking, he flicked the ball past the keeper into the Derby net.

Before I could pull myself up off the ground, Paul was already jumping on top of me. Our small, but insanely devoted traveling supporters were pouring over with excitement . . . literally. I was three feet away from the wall and they were crawling over it, trying to grab anyone they could get their hands on. There was almost a stampede, the security guards came in, and we had to help them break it up. The game was won and I was named Man of the Match.

When I got back home that night the replay of my goal was being played over and over on all the TV highlight shows. I was still completely wired so I called my then-girl-friend—now wife—Cindi, who was at school at the University of Virginia. She'd just finished dinner, picked up the phone, and I started yelling, "Listen! Listen to the TV!" I had the TV blasting and the telephone held up to the speaker so she could hear the highlight. She must have thought I'd lost my mind. I was screaming over the blaring TV set, "Did you hear that? I scored a goal!" This was not the first goal I'd scored in my life and I could tell she had no idea what I was going on about. But no one could have unless they'd seen it themselves. "Oh, uh, that's great, John . . . " And I kept trying to explain, "No, I don't think you *understand.* I scored one of the best goals I've ever scored in my life, in my third start, in a League Cup match, against the most-capped goalkeeper of all time! In the world! PETER SHILTON!" But there was no way to explain what I was feeling right then, by myself, in that little hotel room. I finally thought that I might actually make it over there.

The next day I was all over the papers: "The Yank Has Arrived," "Yank's a Million, Harkes." And, because it was the holiday season, "Harkes the Herald Angel Sings!" Until that point, there had been a few articles that may have mentioned my name in passing, but that was it. And in 1990, soccer made its way into the papers in the States only if the latest badminton championship was canceled. So the attention blew me away. After that goal, the papers kept calling the club asking, "Where the hell has this kid been? Can he shoot like that again?" Of course, there were two sides to it: the attention was great, but from then on, everybody would be watching me more closely. Atkinson was pretty laid back about the whole thing, as any good coach should be. He just said, "Well done, lad. Let's see if you can still do it in training." Of course, when Gary Newbon from ITV asked him about my goal after the game, he replied sarcastically, "Harkesy does the same thing every day in training—no problem."

After that night, that was it. I went from being an American trying to get a regular spot in the starting lineup to being written about, talked about, known. If I had to name one turning point in my career, that goal was it.

It happened so suddenly that I don't really think most people who know me now have any idea what it took just to get me on the field in that one game. I think the public sees my life and my career today and thinks that I just hopped on a plane, kicked the ball around for some people, got signed, and made it—simple as that. But I didn't make it like that. Not even close. I was over there for five months before I ever signed a contract. And even after I signed, I spent most of my time wondering if I'd done the right thing or if I'd end up riding the bench until I went home to the States where I would have no real league to play in.

It's hard to understand how important that time was to me as a person and as a player. And although it was hard at times, my experiences in England would not be the most difficult I had to survive in my career. But they did help prepare me to handle the worst. If I hadn't made it in England, I don't know what I would be doing with my life right now. No clue—none whatsoever.

I have seen a lot of players who decide to go overseas, to England or another country, to try and make it. And it's hard to say why someone does or doesn't succeed. I'll be the first to admit that I was very fortunate that season. I was on a team that was playing well and I was playing well. But I had to work for it. Before and after that night, I was still an outsider in that league and in that country. I still had to prove to players, fans, and coaches, that not only *could* I stick it out, but that they should want me to.

The bar had been raised and the stakes were higher. I was happy to trade my anonymity for increased responsibility and expectations, believe me. But there were a lot more English ready to believe the match that night against Derby was a complete fluke than there were people willing to believe that it was just a good night for an American kid who knew how to play soccer.

This chapter is dedicated to the loving memory of
Victor Cochrane, Robert (Pugsy) Davidson, and Drew Ingles.

Standing on the back line of the Thistle under-19 team, my older brother, Jimmy, and Stuart McEwan's older brother, Scott, were like the Twin Towers. Both 6'3", they were terrifying, they were talented, and no one wanted to go near them with the ball. Thistle was the name of our club teams in Kearny, New Jersey, and when I was 15, the under-16s and under-19s met in the semifinals for the New Jersey state championship. There was sibling rivalry and pride on top of the usual insane level of Kearny-style competition, a must-win for everyone playing. It was brother pitted against brother, and it was fierce.

The game took place at Gunnell Oval, which was a complete dust bowl. Once the game got started, the field had a brown cloud hanging over it, which is not exactly what you want when you're running for 90 minutes. The entire town of Kearny knew about the match and over a thousand people showed up to watch. My dad was coaching my team; Charlie McEwan, father of Stuart and Scott, was coaching my brother's team. My sister, Debbie, was in the stands. And mothers like mine, with a son on each team, were torn and didn't know who to pull for. They sat on the sidelines with

Double-teamed at Kearny High School.

their eyes covered, hoping their boys would come through in one piece.

I really dreaded going up against my brother because he was a tough defender. Jimmy would take down anybody who ran near him—a powerful tackler who won the ball every time. He also read the game very well. And he always challenged me, in particular. He would tackle me hard and then pick me up off the ground saying, "Get up, let's go. Keep playing." Easy for him to say.

As cocky as my friends and I were, especially at 15, we knew we were in for it. So going into the game, my dad's strategy was simple: "You know what they're all about. Don't force it down the middle, and don't hold the ball too long because you'll get hammered. Just keep the ball out wide, and keep it moving—use one and two touches."

Right from the first whistle, players were getting stuck into tackles and bodies were flying everywhere. My brother and his friends were bigger and stronger, and also understood the game better than we did. But we had skill and the fighting underdog mentality—we were scrappy. We had the little

Tony Meola and I: from Kearny High to MLS All-Stars.

feet, the little touches, and we were not intimidated. The crowd never stopped screaming and the ref had his hands full.

Our skill and quickness made up for a lot, and the game went to penalties. We won and earned our bragging rights, but I was too scared to say anything. Debbie was stuck in the middle, congratulating me and consoling Jimmy. After I got home that night and cleaned myself up, I felt like I had just played in an English FA Cup final. But it was just another day in Kearny.

People wonder what makes a town like Kearny such a center for soccer, or Northern Virginia, or St. Louis, or any of the other cities in America that seem to have more than their share of soccer players and fans. In places like these, more kids play soccer today than play Little League baseball. Kearny had baseball fields, too. But we played soccer on them.

It's no coincidence that three U.S. National Team players—Tab Ramos, Tony Meola, and I—grew up playing soccer in the same small town in northern New Jersey, earning

Kearny the title of "SoccerTown, U.S.A." The Kearny formula for success is simple: It's a love for the game. It's a passion, a desire, and a drive—OK, a madness, maybe—that's part of the culture and gets passed down from generation to generation. It's a community that supports the kids who play the sport, and parents, brothers, and sisters who know and follow the game. It's hearing the latest World Cup qualifying match being debated in the street, at school, and in the local bars instead of March Madness or the pennant race. While Kearny is an immigrant community that seems to be a bit behind the times to many outsiders, the town has always been strides ahead of the rest of this country when it comes to developing soccer players.

Growing up in Kearny was a lot like growing up in Europe, as far as soccer was concerned, because of the strong immigrant influence. The town itself was not that big—only about 35,000 people live there. Kearny is a blue-collar town, and when I was a kid, most of the population was Scottish, with some English and Irish mixed in too. Many of our parents came over in the 1950s and '60s to work in the factories that had sprung up near town, or they were the friends and families of workers and earlier immigrants who wanted to live in a community with people they knew from back home.

My mom, Jessie, came to the United States to be a nanny for a family on Long Island, New York. And my dad, Jimmy, came over at 22 after serving in the British Army for two years. He went to Detroit first, for about six months, and then to New York City to find work. He eventually settled in Kearny like the rest of the Scots. Since then, my dad's done construction and worked as a carpenter, which has been his trade since he was 15. He has an eye for things—on a construction site and on the soccer field.

Kearny's not exactly a boomtown and it's always been hard to find work. My parents arrived in this country, and like a lot of immigrants trying to start a new life, they worked nonstop. But they didn't always have a steady income coming into the house. My mom had to work long hours to make sure we had enough money to get by when my dad was be-

1983–84 Kearny High School, with me second from left in the top row.

tween jobs—in a factory, as a secretary, now as a nurse's assistant—while keeping an eye on three kids. But my parents always managed to pull things together for us. And that's the example they set for Jimmy, Debbie, and me. Nothing is going to be handed to you. You have to work for what you want.

That's the way it was for most of my friends, too. My childhood buddies have stayed with me all my life: Rob McCourt, Pete Gaynor, Mike O'Neill, Thomas McKeown, Billy Galka, Larry Hart, Billy Leahy, Phil Downey, Robert Craig, Tommy Mara, Jimmy Byrnes, Ian Gilmartin, Sean McGlynn, and others. I know that sounds like roll call at Ellis Island, but they all have to be mentioned because we were really tight. They were, and are, the best friends anyone could ever want. We started playing together as kids kicking balls around on the playgrounds, then at school, on club teams, and in thousands of pickup games in between. We had something that was, and still is, hard to find in this country. We grew up in a town where soccer was the number one sport for everyone: kids, parents, people in their 20s and 30s, all generations. Even our dads had played together, back in the '60s:

19

Robert's dad, Harry McCourt; Mike's dad, Mike senior; Robert Craig's dad, Bobby; Phil Downey's dad, Ray; Thomas McKeown's dad, Sonny; Tommy Mara's dad, Tom, Sr.; and of course my dad. And when they got older, they coached our club teams, the Thistle.

Each ethnic group had their own social club, and my family lived down the street from the Scots American Club, the meeting place of the Kearny club teams. My mom actually met my dad at a Scot's Club social. The Scots Club had a large downstairs area, a banquet room upstairs, and, of course, a TV over the bar for watching football games. Friends and family in Scotland would sometimes tape the weekly league matches and send the tapes over the next day so that Kearny was never more than a week behind the Scottish football schedule. And from the time I was 5 until I left for college, my club teams would meet at the Scots Club to have pregame talks and get changed into our strips.

Our club team was called Thistle because for years it was sponsored by Thistle Fish and Chips, which was owned by Billy Leahy's dad, Jerry. Jerry and his restaurant have contributed a lot to Kearny soccer. Thistle was structured like a professional club overseas and was pretty elaborate for a town the size of Kearny. From the under-8s to the under-19s and the men's senior team, you moved up through the ranks and developed as a player. I usually played with guys older— and bigger—than I was. Jimmy is three years older than I am, and whatever Jimmy did, I wanted to do too. Wherever he went, I was right on his heels. A bit of a pain in the butt. But playing with him and watching him play gave me a head start on my game, and gave me something to strive for.

My dad coached me at the youth level, and he's had more influence on me as a player than anyone else. I first remember my dad coaching my brother's 7–10 team, the Spurs, and I always tagged along when they would go to practice or games at Gunnell Oval, begging them to let me play. "Too young," I was told. My dad would stand on the sidelines, trying to coach, and I'd be right there under his feet. He'd trip over me, glare down at me and, before I could even ask, he'd say, "No, son. You can't play!" But one day he threw me one of the team's bright orange shirts and said, "All right, go ahead—get on for five minutes, quick. *Don't tell your mother.*" And I went out there, shirt down to my knees, wearing an old pair of my brother's white soccer shoes with red-and-blue stripes. They were way too big for me so I stuffed the toes with newspaper. I looked like Bozo the Clown.

I was 4½, and I thought I was so cool.

We were lucky to have been organized and coached by people who knew the game as well as our fathers did, because even with the huge number of kids playing soccer in the U.S. today, experienced coaches are hard to find—at every level. Our parents also did everything they could to make sure that we had the opportunity not just to play, but to play competitively. We traveled out of town a lot, and it was a big sacrifice because it required time and money. But their efforts paid off, and Kearny started putting out some great players. One of them was Tab Ramos.

I met Tab when I was in junior high. His family had been in the area for about a year when we first heard about him. Everyone, my dad and Mr. Craig especially, was talking about the kid from Uruguay. "Somehow, we have to get him into the Thistle organization," Mr. Craig kept saying. But when Mr. Craig finally did get a hold of Tab, he didn't speak much English. So we told Mr. Craig to start looking for an interpreter to play for the team as well.

Tab and I started out playing against each other, because he was on the other Thistle team in my division. Even though the series stayed pretty even, he was always *the* competition. But I couldn't dislike him—he was just too good. It's no surprise that he went on to play in Spain and Mexico, in three consecutive World Cups, and is regarded as the most skilled player the United States has ever produced. That little touch and flair that he has today as a professional, he had back then as a kid. We always put our biggest, strongest player, Sonny Arena, on him, to try and knock him off the ball. If we could mark Tab out of the game, we stood a chance at winning.

Tony Meola was another great Kearny soccer player. Tony

Big ball, wee man!

was a few years younger than me and lived at the other end of town. But he did play in the Thistle organization, which is how we met. Tony and I didn't play together on the same team until I was a junior and he was a freshman at Kearny High. Even back then, Tony was very athletic and had a lot of confidence—qualities that have made him a great goalkeeper and infuriated many opponents.

But as intense as the club team system was, and as successful as Kearny schools were, the heart of Kearny soccer was the pickup scene. The only thing it can be compared to, really, is inner-city basketball. You had control of the court until you were beat. It was playground against playground. Today, everything is almost too organized. A $60 uniform doesn't make you a player. It's your desire to play the game. We played on asphalt, dirt, and in parking lots. When you have to fight to get a game on a run-down, beat-up court, you're not going to take that time for granted. Pickup is also where players develop their own style, skill, and flair, because they have more freedom to try different things. There were close to 35 of us who would go out and play almost every single day.

When I was in junior high, we played a lot of pickup at my school, Washington. We'd play before school from 8:15 to 8:55. Lunch was from 12:00 to 1:00, and we'd eat for about 15 minutes before heading out to play from 12:15 to 1:00. After school, the high school kids would come down and we'd play from 3:15 to dark. We also played a lot of pickup at Emerson Courts, an arena for street hockey that was solid concrete with a fence around it. A typical Emerson day went something like this: First, Robbie, Mike, and I would meet at Stash's Sub House on Kearny Avenue, where we would down one of the best subs known to man, a bag of Doritos, and a Clinton's Ice Tea—made only in Newark, New Jersey. Then we'd walk up Kearny Avenue a couple of miles to the other side of town, and hook up with Pete Gaynor, Thomas, Galka, and the rest of the boys. By the time we'd walked all the way to Emerson, we'd digested our subs and were ready to play.

At Emerson, everyone divided up into teams of five, and then it was challenge court. You waited your turn to play, and whichever team won got to stay on. If your team got beat at Emerson on a Saturday, you wouldn't get on for at least another hour. When we were freshman, Mike O'Neill would sometimes con the older guys into taking us on. He would say, "Hey, c'mon, look how small we are. You can take us." There was usually a wager involved, and it was at Emerson that Mike earned the name, "Let's Make a Deal" O'Neill. Mike's victims could never believe that a group of youngsters had the ability to beat them at anything. But even though we usually won, it was a very different game at 13 years old, playing against seniors in high school. They were obviously stronger, which meant we got knocked on our butts. Frequently.

I never got tired of playing. I'd be kicking it around out at Emerson and suddenly realize that the street lights were coming on at about 7:00 or 7:30, and I was supposed to have been home at 6:00. I'd come in with skinned knees and scuffed shoes, and my mom would start in about how I should stick to playing against kids my own age and size. But I was always a fearless player. I was going into tackles that people tried to avoid. It was part of the fighting attitude that I carried onto the field. As an adult, I'm still not afraid to get in people's faces, make the hard tackle, and protect my team-mates, but I've had to learn to play smarter and pick my battles.

My first year at Kearny High I was the only freshman on a varsity squad otherwise made up entirely of juniors and se-niors—including my brother. Jimmy was the big man on the team and everybody gave me a hard time because I was the kid brother, the "wee man." I also asked for it. On the field, I was constantly having to prove myself to them as a player. And off the field, I always had to be on my guard because ini-tiation was a very big part of Kearny High soccer.

For a year it was nonstop. I was tied up in an equipment bag and left hanging on a hook in the basement changing room of the Scots Club. I was dragged through the halls of Kearny High by my feet and through the mud puddles after rainy trainings. And the day the guys decided to lock me in my locker, *I* was the one who had to run extra laps. While I was trapped, the rest of the team had gone to start practice— without bothering to tell the coaches why I wasn't out there with them.

But it was all in good fun, and it was all part of the experience and the tradition. I was brought up to respect the older players and coaches. And I learned that respect the old school way. The experience was good for me and it toughened me up. We were successful because playing soccer meant everything to us, and because our coaches understood who we were and where we were coming from. That's why we played so well for them. Coach Millar and Coach Rusek weren't easy on us, that's for sure. But coaches aren't supposed to baby you, they're supposed to push you. And though they gave us a hard time, they were always there for us too, both on and off the field, even when we weren't playing for them. It was just the right balance between challenge and support.

During my four years at Kearny High, we made it to the state championship every year and won three out of four times—including my freshman year. My junior year was a big disappointment; we lost in the final to Toms River High, another Jersey soccer power. But we took the title back my senior year, posting a 24–0 record. We were ranked the number one high school team in the country, and I was named National High School Player of the Year.

The state titles and recognition that the team earned at Kearny High were incredible, and the whole town threw their support behind us. We had police escorts from games, parades, and the most devoted fans anywhere. The team's reputation also helped get players recognized by college coaches with scholarships to give out. But if a player really wanted to get noticed by the U.S. Soccer Federation—something that was key for anyone wanting a serious future as a player—he had to make it through state and regional tryouts.

Each year there were tryouts for regional and state teams, the first step toward working your way into the Olympic Development Program and eventually getting recognized by U.S. Soccer and having a shot at a youth national team. At the state level, tryouts were huge; hundreds of kids would show up. If you made it through to the next round, you'd go to another town and do it all over again until the final cut was made. My friends and I used to have to jog down to Highway 280 to get picked up by the closest available carpool going to training and games.

My junior year, we had tryouts at Great Gorge. We loved to travel up to Great Gorge because the facilities were so much better than what we were used to. There was always a big crew of players from Kearny High and Thistle who made it to the tryouts—the fact that there were so many of us, year after year, said a lot about the quality of soccer in Kearny. And that year 10 Thistle players ended up being selected. Unfortunately, the same weekend as the tryouts, my Thistle team was scheduled to play in a New Jersey State Cup quarterfinal match. My dad had to have us there for that game or else he wouldn't have had a real team. He called Chuck Blazer, then with the New Jersey State Soccer Association, and tried to get the game rescheduled, but Blazer told him to talk to the coach of the opposing team. Of course, the other coach said that the game would go on as scheduled, and if my dad couldn't produce his full team, Thistle would have to forfeit.

So my dad called Manny Schellscheidt, another topnotch coach, who was running the tryouts at Great Gorge, and asked if he could have us for one morning during the weekend of tryouts, but Manny said no. He told my dad that we were doing well and would probably advance to the next round of tryouts, so leaving was out of the question. My dad promised to bring us back as soon as it was done, but Manny wouldn't change his mind. The State Cup meant everything to us, so we wanted to leave. But, at the same time, I didn't want to blow a chance to get into the National Team system. It was like the ongoing conflicts between the U.S. National Team and Major League Soccer (MLS) that some players have today, only on a smaller scale. Even back then we were torn between our loyalties to different teams.

So my dad and Pete Gaynor's dad, Joe, did what they had to do for the sake of the team: they drove up to Great Gorge in Joe's station wagon and kidnapped us in the middle of the night. We snuck out of the dorm, piled in the car, drove all night, and got back to my house, where my mom had a big Scottish breakfast waiting for us.

Thistle won the game 3–1, and a couple of us still got picked to go through to the next round of the state tryouts. But that was the kind of commitment that our families and the Kearny community made to soccer. Everyone in my family understood how important it was to me. Even my sister, Debbie, who only played soccer for a year herself, always came to the games and supported Jimmy and me whenever we played. It was hard at times for her, I'm sure, because my life, our family, and the entire town of Kearny, was so soccer "daft," as the Scots would say. But she was, and always has been there for me, and always understood how important soccer was in my life.

Every summer, Kearny soccer fans turned out in the thousands when the youth teams of Celtic's football club in Scotland came over to play the Thistle teams. It was the highlight of the soccer year. They called it the Celtic Boys Tour, and the teams played games all over the country. But they always saved their last match for Kearny. These were 14-, 15-, 16-year-old kids who, if they were good enough, started professional careers in Scotland at 17, so we had the chance to go up against future pros. I played against guys like Paul McStay, Tony Shepard, and Peter Grant when I was 14 years old. I also played against Owen Archdeacon, who would eventually play against me in England when he was with Barnsley. The turnouts we got for those matches 15 years ago were more impressive than the numbers you see for most college soccer games today—3,000 or 4,000 people crowded around a soccer field in Kearny. Of course, a lot of people who lived in Kearny were cheering for Celtic and against us. But that's just how it was. A lot of them had grown up with Celtic, and it was in their blood, if not their religion. In Glasgow, when Celtic, the Catholic club, play against Rangers, the Protestant club, sports and religion overlap in one of the most passionate rivalries in sports. So it was nearly impossible to get Celtic fans to turn against their club, even if it was in support

*My dad, Jimmy, second from left on top, with
Kearny Scots oldtimers team.*

of the local kids team. Beating them meant a lot because we
had to prove ourselves to the Celtic supporters in Kearny.

Year after year, Celtic won. When I was 15, my dad was finally given the chance—after six years of coaching Kearny's
club teams—to select and coach the team that would represent Kearny against Celtic. And that summer, we beat them
for the first time ever, winning 3–1. We proved that we were
on par with some of the best young players in the world; that
we could compete with a European club. We proved to our
town and to a European side that we could beat Celtic's best.
My dad was so proud of us—the whole town was—and I was
proud of him, too.

Whether or not he was coaching me, my dad taught me a
lot of little lessons. But he always did it subtly. He left final
decisions about my life and my playing up to me, never told
me what to do, and he never pressured me to play soccer. He

was always quite a critic, but his opinion was more important to me than any coach's. After every game, when I came home, I immediately wanted to know what my dad thought. But he would never come right out and tell me. He would sit there, reading his paper, doing the crossword puzzle, or watching a game. And if I wanted him to say something I'd have to pull it out of him.

Even if I thought I'd played really well, I'd come in and look for him, to hear what *he* thought. But he wouldn't say a word. So I'd finally say, "Well, what do you think?" And he'd say something like, "I thought it was a good game today."

"No, I mean, how do you think *I* played?" Then there would be a long pause.

"Well, I guess you did all right."

"What do you mean—all right?"

"Well, first half, you lost the ball." And as he's saying this, he's still looking at the paper or watching the TV.

"Yeah, I remember. But dad, come on. I was doing everything. I was . . . " and then I'd ramble on about my play.

"Yeah, I know son, you're doing well, but I don't think you're there yet. Simple passes, John, that's what it's all about. Simple passes," he said, and always with a big smile on his face. I loved him for that.

And that would be it. I always left those conversations thinking, "I've got to get better." He always had a way of making me want to work harder, even when he hinted slyly that he thought I'd played well. Even now he can tell when I'm off my game. He'll say, "You don't look like you're focused, I can tell. You need to get back on your game."

My friends are the same way. It doesn't matter that I'm a pro player now, or what kind of experience I have. They know if I'm on my game. And if I'm not, they'll just say, "Been a little quiet lately, Harkesy." That's why they're true friends—because they're honest. But on my game or not, they were also true friends because they stuck by me, and they have continued to do so for years.

And you needed true friends like that in Kearny—friends who would tell it to you straight—because Kearny could be pretty tough. The attitude I had was the kind that is usually associated with kids from New York and Jersey: that city-kid edge, never backing down. But the facts were, you either learned to fend for yourself or you got pushed around. When I look back on it now, I think maybe I used my wit and my attitude to make up for my size, or maybe I was doing it to prove I could run with the older guys who were always bigger and tougher. And it's still a challenge now, as an adult, not to always react in that same Kearny way when I'm in a difficult situation.

I'm glad I wasn't spoiled. I always had to work for spending money—catering fish and chips for the Thistle, working construction with my dad, cleaning out ovens in a jewelry factory. That's what my parents drilled into me. And I think that work ethic has carried over into my playing career. My coaches and the media have always said that the strength of my game is my work rate. Having to work for everything as a kid didn't just make me appreciate what I had, it also made me realize that I definitely didn't want to spend my life struggling to get by. I had to do everything I could to succeed in soccer.

But it wasn't easy. It was a rough area, and there were a lot of distractions growing up. We were brought up in an atmosphere where alcohol was socially acceptable, even at 14 or 15. It was everywhere, all the time, and we didn't know any other way of life. And when you're in high school, you think you're invincible. It wasn't until I left Kearny that I realized how easily my life could have gone in another direction. But soccer helped keep us grounded, and it saved a lot of us. I know it saved me. My friends and I might go out and get into trouble, but we never wanted anything to keep us from playing. We might stay out late at night, but we'd never sleep late and miss a match. We helped keep each other in line.

Even though I wanted my soccer playing to help me get out of Kearny, it was easy to get comfortable there, too. I had great friends, more soccer than I had time to play, and I was surrounded by people I'd known all my life who came from

My parents (on my right) and I, along with Mike O'Neill and his mother
at the Fred L. Coggins awards ceremony in 1984.

the same background that I did. Those reasons kept a lot of
talented players there, players who never had the chance to
go all the way with their game and see where it could take
them. It wasn't something that surprised me, because I came
close to making the same choice myself. But the Kearny boys
would have never let me stay—it would have been an insult
to everything we dreamed about and worked for together as
players and as friends. Our generation was really the first
given an opportunity to leave Kearny, and soccer was our
ticket out. Robert left for Adelphi. Mike went to Old Domin-
ion. Pete went to St. Peters and later transferred to ODU, as
well.

I knew I would miss those friends, my family, and my
town. But I also knew that they would always be there for
me. And growing up seeing the drinking, the drugs, the unemployment, and the constant struggles that all our families
had to deal with every day, I knew that if soccer could get me
away from that environment, even for a little while, I had to
go.

L ying in bed, getting prepped for my surgery, I was starting to get woozy. Bruce Arena, my coach at the University of Virginia, was sitting on the end of my bed in blue hospital scrubs saying, "Everything will be OK, John. You're gonna be fine." Seeing Bruce in that gear, I remember laughing to myself, "Wow—I'm glad he's not my doctor . . . "

I was thankful, though, that Bruce had offered to come with me, because having another person in the room helped take my mind off my situation. Just months before I was supposed to start training for a spot on the 1988 Olympic team, I turned for a ball during practice and felt something snap. Our assistant coach, Dave Sarachan, was standing next to me when it happened and said, "Something didn't sound right." That "something" was the fifth metatarsal of my left foot, and it needed a pin. The operation on my foot would very likely wreck what might be my only chance ever to be an Olympian. I was not happy.

Bruce was encouraging, and said it was an easy operation—"You'll be in and out, no problem." But the last thing I remember Bruce saying to me as I drifted off was, "Don't worry—I'll look after you."

"Great . . . " I mumbled, laughing, as the anesthetic kicked in. Then I was out.

When I woke up, Dr. McCue was standing over me, but Bruce was nowhere to be seen. "You seem to be the better patient," Dr. McCue said, "Bruce had a little accident."

Bruce wanted to watch the surgery—smock, mask, gloves, and all—and apparently he made it all the way through, but as soon as the doctors closed up the incision, he passed out cold, knocking over an entire tray of medical instruments. Dr. McCue said he was OK.

The next day, when I saw Bruce, he didn't say anything about his "little accident." I brought it up, of course, and all he said was, "It was nothing. I just kinda tripped." He was kidding, as usual. Although often perceived as standoffish, Bruce is capable of delivering some classic one-liners—usually in that know-it-all New York accent of his—and he's always good for a laugh. It wasn't the only time that Bruce would be there for me . . . or pass out in front of me.

Bruce first saw me play as a freshman at Kearny High. But it was Dave Sarachan—Bruce's assistant while he was with D.C. United—who made the first recruiting trip to Jersey my senior year. When I walked into the school counselor's office to meet with him, I was a sight, wearing black pinstripe jeans, a gray pinstripe shirt, black Capezio shoes, and a skinny black leather tie. I thought I was John Travolta from the movie *Saturday Night Fever,* but was far from it because I did my shopping at Chess King. God knows what Dave was thinking then (he told me a year later he wondered if he had the right kid). But once he saw me out on the field, that was enough to get Bruce to come up for a visit with my family.

He came to the house, sat down in the living room, and told us what the University of Virginia had to offer. I didn't need to be sold on UVA academically, but as far as soccer was concerned, I was seriously considering some other schools, especially North Carolina State. N.C. State was appealing to me because Tab Ramos was there and I knew he liked their soccer program. It wasn't the head coach, Larry Gross, that impressed Tab or me, but George Tarantini, his assistant.

Tarantini was also the under-16 regional coach at the time. It was clear my parents liked Bruce a lot and liked UVA's academic reputation, and I did too. On the other hand, having Tab vouch for a program was a plus. My head was spinning. It was a big decision for me, and one I assumed I'd have to live with for the next four years.

The decision was particularly difficult because I wasn't always sure college was the right choice for me as a soccer player. It certainly wasn't a part of the plan for serious footballers in Europe. I remembered all the kids from Celtic that I'd played against growing up and how, right after high school, they were going on trials with any club that would take a look at them. But unless I left the country after high school—which I sometimes wish I had—a good collegiate soccer program was the best thing I could do for my career, especially with no professional league in the States at the time. So I eventually decided to go to UVA. Coach Tarantini was a class act and wished me luck, Bruce seemed pleased, and I was relieved to know where I would be going, come fall.

When I got down to UVA, Bruce took a special interest in me and helped me adjust to a new and different environment. Bruce also knew that I was a soccer player going to college and that if the right chance presented itself I wouldn't be there for long. Still, he gave me an opportunity that helped me to mature as a person and as a player, and for that reason UVA was a valuable stepping-stone.

We had a talented group of players my freshman year that included Sean McGlynn, who had played with me on Thistle, Bob Willen, Drew Fallon, Dave Mancuso, George Gelnovatch, and Jeff Gaffney. And we were surrounded by excellent coaches: Bruce, Dave Sarachan, and Craig Reynolds. Just like at Kearny High, I was a freshman playing on the varsity squad and I wanted to make a difference. But this was another level, and I wondered if I would be able to start and make an impact right away. I wanted to make my mark.

So in my first practice at UVA, I knocked our star forward, Jeff Gaffney, on his butt. I wasn't looking to do it, I just got caught up in the run of play and it happened. Bruce told me later that he knew then I would be able to take care of myself. Of course, I think it was after that same practice that Bruce strolled up to me, after I'd showered and gotten dressed, and said, "Hey Harkes, I see you got rid of your skinny leather tie."

I knew then that Bruce and I would hit it off.

Bruce wanted us to enjoy playing, and even though he was a very serious coach, he knew how to have a good time. He would often join in at the end of training and goof around with the players, something he also did occasionally at D.C. United. But of all the practices during my years at UVA, the day before our opener against Notre Dame my first year stands out above the rest.

We were working on penalty kicks, when Bruce walked over and announced to the team, "The best way to take a penalty is German. The Bundesliga penalty kick."

So he stepped up and cracked the hell out of the ball. Right after he took the shot, he turned to look back at us, and then collapsed. Laughing, Dave Sarachan ran up to him and yelled, "Bruce . . . Bruce . . . Can ya talk to me? Talk to me Bruce . . . " But he wasn't moving. After a few moments we realized that Bruce wasn't kidding—he was out cold. The next thing we knew, the trainers were running onto the field to revive him. When Bruce had struck the ball, he pulled his quad in the process and the pain was so intense it caused him to pass out. When he finally started to come to, he was pretty groggy. He slowly picked up his head, looked around, and then he fell back on the grass. Pat Mugler and Dave Mancuso, reserves at the time, decided this was the perfect time to send Bruce subliminal messages. They stood above him repeating, "Play Mancuso and Mugler, play Mancuso and Mugler . . ." Even though Bruce was in agony, we couldn't help but laugh. This time, I was awake for the whole thing and none of us ever let him forget it.

Although Bruce liked my fighting spirit and tenacity, he never wanted my temper to interfere with my play. So when I head-butted a Clemson player five games into my first sea-

Junior year at UVA.

son, Bruce took me aside. "John," he said seriously, "You're playing great for us, but you gotta minimize the head-butting business." But overall, I knew he was pleased. I was stepping up, and he let me play my game.

We won the first 12 games of the season and I played most of it as a defensive midfielder, creating and playing balls out of the back, feeding Gaffney and Gelnovatch up front. When it came time for the NCAA playoffs, we had to face George Mason, the team we'd lost to 3–2 in the last regular season match. We were heavily favored going into the game, but ended up losing 1–0. After such a successful season, it was bitterly disappointing to get knocked out of the tournament so early on. We knew we had the talent to go all the way, but our shot at a national championship would have to wait until the following year.

In the summer of 1986 I attended the Olympic Festival in

Houston and was the youngest member on the East squad. It was there that I met my future wife, Cindi Kunihiro. Cindi was an alternate on the women's East soccer team, and luckily for me, she got called up for the Festival at the last minute. Fate. I chased her down—literally—while all the teams were walking around the track of the Astrodome during the opening ceremonies. After "catching up" to her there, I tried to run into her every chance I had. We hit it off, I convinced her to give me her address, and we kept in touch throughout the summer. Even though we were away from each other a lot because of all my traveling, I was convinced we would make it work. Twelve years and two children later, it looks like we have.

Professionally speaking, we—the East—won the "Festival" gold that summer. And that was the first time Bob Gansler, who was full-time National Team coach at the time, got a good look at me as a player and started thinking about bringing me into the U.S. Men's training camp. It was a big step to go from the youth level to the full national side, and I was excited about the prospect of making it.

The following year, UVA had another top recruiting class, which included Jeff Agoos, who would later be my teammate on both D.C. United and the U.S. National Team. Bruce let me know at the beginning of the season that he wanted me to move forward a lot more that year, and I was looking forward to it. I loved getting into the attack and it showed. I finished the season with nine goals, up from two my freshman year. As a team, we built on the success we'd had the previous year and we finished out the season on a 16-game winning streak. We went into the NCAA tournament ranked #1 in the country, but we weren't any more successful than we'd been the year before. We were taken out, 1–0, by Loyola College of Maryland, a team we were expected to walk over on our way to the second round. The press, the school, Bruce, but especially the players, wondered why, with such a talented team, we couldn't win when it really mattered.

Christmas came and went, and in January of 1987, I was the youngest player called in by Bob Gansler to train with the

National Team. That was when I first met "Sully," Christopher Sullivan, who is still a good friend of mine. Sully was older, more experienced, and I looked up to him. He was also one of the first players to make it in Europe, where he played in Hungary with Raba Eto. Mike Windischmann, who had been with me during the 1986 Olympic Festival, was there, too. Sully and Windy made my first nerve-wracking experience with the U.S. team much easier to handle and a lot more fun.

I got my first official cap that spring in an Olympic qualifying match against Canada. I was 20 years old. Playing for the National Team had been a goal of mine for as long as I could remember, and I finally had my chance. I started in five consecutive games for the U.S. before heading back to Virginia in the fall. I felt I was finally working my way into a regular spot on the squad and I was also on track to compete in the 1988 Olympics.

My junior year, 1987–1988, was hectic. Virginia had the #1 soccer program in the country at the time, and as a result, a lot of quality players were coming to play there: Tony Meola, John Maessner, Kris Kelderman, and Curt Onalfo to name a few. And, Cindi was recruited by the women's team. I was psyched because she was thinking about going to Cornell or Harvard. Academically, Virginia was on par with many Ivy League schools, but UVA had the better soccer program. Cindi had been playing with the under-19 National Team that summer and wanted to continue to compete against top players, most of whom were in UVA's conference. I was happy that we could finally be together.

That year, Bruce made me captain, I scored 15 goals during the season, and I received the Missouri Athletic Club's Player-of-the-Year award. I felt like I'd come a long way in three years. In the time that I had been at UVA, the soccer program had gone from good to unbeatable—for the most part—and it was exciting to play a key part in the building of Virginia's soccer dynasty. It helped that I was surrounded by great teammates and good coaches. At the end of the season, the Cavs were still ranked #1 and were again headed to the

Bruce (center) with Bob Willen and I receiving Goalkeeper of the Year and Missouri Athletic Club's Player of the Year, respectively.

NCAA tournament as big favorites. I thought for sure this was our year. But we lost to Loyola—again—this time in the second round. I began to wonder if I would ever wear a championship ring.

On the upside, my chances looked good to earn a spot on the 1988 Olympic squad. Tab was going to be there, and so were Windy and Sully. I couldn't wait. Then I broke my foot and it looked like my Olympic dreams were shattered.

Bruce, Dr. McCue, and I decided that with the number of games I had coming up, putting the pin in would be the wisest thing to do. The surgery was harder on me mentally than it was physically—although Bruce's collapse did a lot to lighten up the procedure itself. But I was completely devastated and couldn't handle the fact that I might have to miss out on the opportunity to represent my country in Seoul. I started rehab as soon as I could, but it took a while to get back on my feet. I was in a lot of pain, but staying home wasn't an option I was willing to consider.

The Olympic team was training in Florida. I went and worked my butt off trying to get fit. One afternoon, Coach Lothar Osiander called me into his room for a talk. He sat me down and I knew he wasn't going to say anything I wanted to hear. He took a breath and said, "Harkesy . . . " And I thought, "Oh my God . . . don't tell me I'm not going." It meant everything to me. "I don't know what to tell you, Harkesy, I just don't know what to tell you. You're still in pain and I have to finalize my 22 soon." And that's when I started to lose it.

"You've got to keep me on the team. I can make it. There's still time and I'll be 100 percent. I'll be ready to step on the field and play for you, for my country. You've got to give me a chance . . . " And he did. Lothar just wanted to hear from *me* that I thought I could make it. He wanted to know that I was willing to fight through the pain and do whatever was necessary. And I was.

At that point, I was still limping and couldn't train with the team. I was off doing my own thing with the trainer, and Lothar even took time out to train me individually.

"Okay, Harkesy, let's fix you up," he'd say. Then it was nonstop running, drills, anything to build my strength back up. And I was doing everything I could to push through the pain. I had to prove to him that I could make it. I was lucky he was willing to invest in my rehab the way that he did, but spending so much time one-on-one with Lothar was an experience in itself. Lothar was known for being a little wacky, and he even showed up for training one day wearing a baseball cap with big "Goofy" ears attached to it. He kept things interesting, and always managed to catch his players off guard.

During one of my workouts with him, Lothar jumped into my arms without any warning and made me carry him up and down the field—his idea of building strength and entertaining the rest of the team. I ran from one end of the field to the other with him in my arms shouting, "Come on, Harkesy! This will get you fit—I know you can make it!" All the other players stopped what they were doing. Tab, Eric Eichmann, Sully, and Windy were gathered at the water cooler, hunched over in hysterics. Tab yelled, " Harkesy, are you kiddin' me?!" I was laughing too—which was making it even harder to keep my balance—and my foot was *killing* me. But I was determined to get fit . . . and I was always good for a laugh. Believe it or not, I actually "broke through" some of the pain that day, something that Dr. McCue told me would eventually happen. Even though I pushed myself, once the Olympics rolled around, I still didn't feel game fit.

But there I was, sitting on the bench in the first game of the Olympics watching us beat Argentina 1–0 in front of a packed house. There were about 10 minutes left to play when Lothar told me to start warming up; I was going in. The U. S. was playing well, but Argentina was a quality team. They were coming back, and we were under a lot of pressure. I wondered if I was sharp enough to go in—not the frame of mind you want to be in when you're getting ready to step on the field for an Olympic match. Argentina showed no signs of slowing and it was clear that the game was far from over.

I had been on the field for less than five minutes when Argentina got the ball and one of their strikers started heading down the wing with it. Paul Caligiuri was marking him, but he got beat and I stepped over to pressure the player. I was inside the 18 and just about to run out to make the tackle when he touched the ball right by me. I stopped to turn and get the ball, and he ran into me, fell over my legs, and hit the ground—professional dive. Penalty. The guy was going for an academy award and had clearly given this performance before. But hey—we've all done it. I was pissed. I managed to come back from my injury, get my big chance, walk into a winning situation, and the next thing I knew I was watching Argentina's penalty shot hit the back of the net. The game ended 1–1, and I didn't think there was any way I would see playing time in another Olympic match. I felt like I'd let the team and Lothar down, and everything was going through my 20-year-old head. At that point, my future with the National Team didn't look too bright.

But when Lothar posted the starting lineup for our next game, against South Korea, I was on it. I had to look twice to make sure. I was completely shocked, and also grateful for a second chance. I think Lothar wanted to see how I would respond and perform after what had happened in the first match. I was ready. The team played well, I played well, and we tied the game 0–0. The next and final game was against Russia. I called Cindi the day before the game and said I was finally feeling good about my place on the team. I told her how much I was looking forward to playing against the Soviet Union. U.S.-U.S.S.R. was, after all, a classic Olympic rivalry. "I think he might start me," I told her. "I played well in the last game."

I was confident, I was psyched, I was benched.

I found out when I got to the stadium. Not only was I not starting, I wasn't even playing. In fact, Tab, Windy, and I had all been dropped from the roster. And we weren't just benched, we had to sit in the stands. Lothar had gone with the older, more experienced players. Even though we lost 4–2, it would have been nice to be on the bench with the rest of the team for our final Olympic experience. None of us ever asked Lothar about it, because we had too much respect for him and the older players, but it was disappointing. They sat us right next to the press, not the most comfortable seats in the house when your team is losing.

Despite leaving Seoul without a medal, I had a tremendous experience and it was an honor to be there. I was also grateful for the chances Lothar gave me, considering my health and that first game. But I also felt it was important to be a part of the Olympics because a large part of the public was still unaware that soccer was even an event. It was another opportunity to raise awareness and to prove to other countries at yet another level of competition that the United States was improving and was determined to be a major player on the world stage.

Before I went back to UVA to start my senior year, it was time for another big decision. Over the summer, the Federation had started talking about signing National Team players to full-time contracts. They wanted the players to devote all their time and energy for the rest of 1988 and 1989 to qualifying for the 1990 World Cup. The U.S. hadn't gone to the World Cup in 40 years. As wonderful an opportunity as it was, playing for the U.S. full-time meant giving up my eligibility at UVA.

So I had to choose between school and soccer. I discussed the situation with my dad, Cindi, Dave Sarachan, and, of course, Bruce. I'd gone to Bruce for advice a lot over the years, about things that had to do with soccer and life in general. I trusted his opinion and I think he understood what was important to me. At the same time, he didn't want to lose me. If I stayed for my senior year, I had a good shot at winning the Hermann Trophy. And there was always the chance that we could finally win the national championship. But my dad and Bruce told me how important it was to team chemistry for a team to stick together through qualifying—something I would remember years later.

Soccer had always been a part of my life, and I wanted it to be my career. But I wanted to make sure I did the right thing and I was struggling with the decision. So I called Cindi, and she came up to Kearny. She knew how much my career at UVA meant to me, but she also realized that playing on the National Team was an honor. She knew that deep down I really wanted to make it at the top level and that this was my chance. She also knew I was ready to move on.

I definitely wanted to be a part of the team that would try to get the United States to its first World Cup in 40 years so I decided to go for it and signed for around $36,000 a year, pocket change compared to the salaries of most professional athletes. But that wasn't important to me. My dream was starting to become a reality.

The small bus we were riding in was surrounded by Trinidad and Tobago supporters as we drove into the stadium in Port of Spain. All I could see was red. Everyone blocking the path of our bus was wearing red. Every person climbing over the stadium wall was wearing red. And every person watching the closed-circuit TV on the hillside overlooking the stadium was wearing red. This was what most of the soccer world got to experience the day of a big game, but we'd never seen anything like it. We were getting a taste of what the World Cup might be like if we qualified. Still, we thought to ourselves, "How are we going to pull this off?"

Qualifying for the 1990 World Cup came down to this very last match, and as soon as we stepped off the plane in Port of Spain it was clear to every player on the National Team that this was not going to be like any other game we'd ever played. Cameras were flashing, TV crews were there, and the T & T supporters were taunting us and singing. We were stunned, but we loved it. A four-day national holiday had been declared: two days before the game, game day, and the day after. The whole country came to a halt.

It had been a long haul getting to this last match. We had played some tough games during qualifying and earned a lot

The "shot heard 'round the world." To my left are
Paul Caliguri, Bruce Murray, Tab Ramos and Peter Vermes.

of draws. At the time, going down to Central America and getting a tie was a great result for us. Every match was do or die, and every trip was unique in its own way. Bad hotel food in one country, getting stuck in an elevator four hours before kickoff in another. And the whole experience was made even more incredible by the presence of Walter Bahr, a member of the history-making 1950 World Cup team that beat England 1–0. Walter traveled with us to almost all the games, and it meant a lot to us to have someone there who had been on the U.S. team the last time we'd qualified for the World Cup. We wanted Walter to be able to see the U.S. get there again.

The day before the game, training was unbearable as we tried to adjust to the heat. And the night before the match, I was too fidgety to sleep. T & T was sure they were going to beat us and be on the way to their first World Cup. The papers, TV, the guy at the bus stop—everyone was predicting 2–0, 3–0. And back then, we knew it would be hard. We were young, and we were playing away against a team with a lot more experience than we had, in front of a crowd we knew would be intense.

At the same time, the intensity got us pumped up and excited, and raised our level of play. No one on the U.S. team really had any idea how to react under those kind of circumstances or what this game would mean to the future of soccer in the States. But that country and their fans woke us up. The atmosphere they created carried us into the game. Sometimes I think if we had played that game at home, we probably would have lost. But the people and the passion of the tiny island got us psyched. We knew we were the underdogs, but we had responded well to that in the past.

Once we saw the scene around and inside the stadium, we actually worried about the security of our families because we had no idea where they would be seated. My mom and dad, Cindi—everybody had come down for the game. It was a relief when I caught sight of them during the "National Anthem": a tiny white corner in a sea of red.

Most games fly by, but I remember a lot about this one. I'll say this: the soccer played that day wasn't very pretty. Technically, our team just wasn't that good. It was also around 100°, and we felt it once the game started. But we ran our hearts out, and late in the first half, it happened: the goal that sent the U.S. to the World Cup for the first time in 40 years. In the 31st minute, Paul Caligiuri unleashed a dipping blast from 30 yards out that would later be known as "the shot heard 'round the world." And with that history-making goal, the little corner of white erupted while the rest of the stadium, the parking lot, the hill—the whole country—sat in a silent state of shock. We were delirious, running all over the field, tackling each other.

For the next 60 or so minutes, we tried to hold onto our 1–0 lead for dear life. Tying was not an option if we wanted to go to the World Cup. We had some chances, played OK at times, and held on. By the time the game was over we were

Taking on Trinidad and Tobago players in the heat.

ecstatic, but completely exhausted. That night, I was too tired to really celebrate. I had lost seven pounds since I'd gotten down there and was drained. Instead of going out on the town, we sat around the hotel pool with family and friends and talked about the match and what had just happened. We couldn't believe we had won and qualified for the World Cup. Once my mind stopped racing, I was finally able to go to sleep.

What we accomplished that day was the first step toward changing the future of soccer here in the States. All of a sudden the U.S. was on the world soccer map. *That's* where it all started: the beginning of an entirely new era for American soccer. Even in the most successful career, it's rare to be involved in such a defining moment, a group achievement that will go down in the books. The 1994 World Cup here in the States was big too, especially from a media standpoint, but as far as turning points in the history of soccer in the United States is concerned, qualifying for the 1990 World Cup was far more significant.

Before that day, going to the World Cup was only a dream and not something I had considered a real possibility. Once we'd made it, it was big news all over the world. Of course, we had no idea whatsoever what the World Cup would be like, on or off the field. We couldn't imagine what it would be like to play at that level.

In January 1990, five months before the World Cup, I went to England on a two-week trial at Sheffield Wednesday, with manager Ron Atkinson. It had been about two months since the final qualifying match against Trinidad and Tobago, and I wasn't match fit. But I was excited. I trained my butt off and, at the end of the two weeks, Ron Atkinson said that he'd like to keep me on loan from the Federation until the World Cup. At that point, Coach Gansler could call me back to the National Team. It was a great opportunity and something I'd always wanted, but I actually turned down Atkinson's offer. We were only six months away from the World Cup, and I didn't want to miss any part of the experience. I also didn't think that it would help me or the team if I (but virtually no one else) was away during the last months of preparation. Fortunately, Atkinson seemed to understand my situation— although he probably didn't agree with my decision—and left open the possibility that I could come back after the World Cup. That opening relieved my anxiety, and I didn't feel like I was "missing out" by not jumping at the offer immediately.

I loved being part of the National Team, getting paid a salary to play soccer and travel around the world. I didn't think life could get any better: $36,000 a year and I thought I was a millionaire. When I wasn't with the National Team, I was back in Jersey hanging out with Robbie, Pete, and the boys, or I'd go down to UVA to see Cindi, driving the '84 Honda I'd saved up for. When I was available, I also played for the Albany Capitals of the American Soccer League. For the time being, my life seemed set.

The team was together for six to eight weeks straight before the World Cup, and Coach Gansler ran a tight ship. He checked what we ate, got mad if we cracked jokes during team meals, wanted it quiet on the bus going to games, and came around knocking on doors when it was curfew time. He wanted us focused and ready.

Before we left for Europe, the Federation had a big send-off for the team in New York City's Little Italy. All the people milling around in the streets and the small, packed Italian restaurants decorated with "Italia '90" paraphernalia made it finally sink in that we were going to the World Cup. On our way there, we stopped and trained in Switzerland for two weeks. There I was treated by a deep-tissue massage specialist from Italy for a slight tear of a stomach muscle that had been giving me trouble. The treatment itself was incredibly painful, but I felt awesome afterward and after a couple days I was back to full training. We worked on team play and tactics and tried to get mentally prepared for the World Cup. We stayed in a beautiful hotel and the scenery was gorgeous: rocks, cliffs, mountains. I was a long way from Jersey.

From Switzerland, we headed down to Tirrenia, Italy, where we were based for most of the tournament. We were expecting to be blown away by the country's passion for soccer and we wanted to be in the thick of everything, as we had been in Trinidad and Tobago. But Tirrenia is a tiny village located on the western coast of Italy, just below Pisa. We were out of the way and staying at a heavily secured dormitory-like army camp. Once, I had to convince the armed security guard—complete with guard dogs—to let me out alone for a few minutes to see Cindi and her brother when they made the journey out to visit me. Because we were so isolated, it took us a while to realize that we were a part of what was taking place. Regardless, the most amazing thing about the 1990 World Cup was that we were there.

Mike Windischmann and I were roommates throughout National Team training camp and during the 1990 World Cup. That's a lot of time to spend in one room with another person, and Windy and I were kind of an odd couple. The musical selection in our room went back and forth between Led Zeppelin and Run DMC. I tried to turn him on to alternative rock, and he did his best to educate me about New York City rap.

Windy was an ideal roommate for me. He was a joker, he loved pranks, and he never seemed to get stressed out. But he also loved to sleep and do his own thing. I, on the other hand, always wanted to go places and be entertained. I go stir-crazy in hotels, so I was a pain in the butt to him, always nagging him to go out and walk around, go to the mall, anything. He was always telling me to shut up so he could sleep. We got into our own kind of a rhythm that way. He would put on his headphones and try to drown me out, while I would watch TV and try to get him to have a chat.

"Windy . . . "

"What do you want?"

"You're a great roommate, you know that? All you do is listen to music all day."

"It's good. You want to hear it?"

"No. Can't you just talk and watch TV?"

"No, because I don't want to watch TV."

"What are you so grumpy about?"

"Shut up or get out, Harkesy, I'm going to sleep." I just chuckled.

The team had a huge amount of respect for Windy. He was a talented sweeper with good vision—the man could pass the ball anywhere—and a valuable captain. He was not very vocal, but when there was something important that needed to be said, Windy would let people know. I was lucky to have him as a roommate. He helped keep my perspective in check and also kept me laughing.

Our big day out we went to the Leaning Tower of Pisa. Tony, Windy, Sully, and I took pictures of each other "holding up" the tower. This was our chance to see our families. When we ventured out we were recognized—probably because we were dressed, head to toe, in U.S. gear—and we were kind of a novelty with the press. But we got our first taste of the World Cup when we traveled to Florence to play Czechoslovakia.

Because we had been kept so isolated, it sometimes felt like we were training for a friendly match at home in the States. Once in Florence we got a good look at the role that soccer plays in Italy's culture, but we didn't have long to adjust to the atmosphere. We were excited, but we weren't quite sure what it would be like to play in front of a World Cup crowd for the first time.

As we stood across midfield and the National Anthem played, I thought, "This is it—we really made it." The game started and we were jittery, unable to get into any kind of a rhythm. In a way, we started out in that first game thinking, "Hey—look at us! We're in the World Cup!" We were like tourists with field access, and we had a nightmare game. We lost Eric Wynalda when he got ejected in the 52nd minute, so we had to play a man down, which didn't make things any easier. When it was all over, we had been schooled by the Czechs 5–1.

The humiliating loss was a big eye-opener: "Welcome to the big time." We went back to camp and regrouped to get ready for our next match, against Italy in Rome. In the days leading up to the match, we started getting more coverage and were on the Italian news almost every night. We were probably the most inexperienced team there, and we were still young, so it caught us off guard to be treated like celebrities. It was amazing to be in a country where football was everything. We had seen our share of soccer-crazed countries during qualifying, especially in Trinidad, but in those countries there wasn't a lot of money put into the sport. It was popular because it was a game of the people—which is still the reason soccer is *the* #1 sport in the world. But the Italian footballers were like rock stars or royalty. I had never seen anything like it.

The opportunity to play the home team—in a country like Italy—took the World Cup experience to another level. Looking out the bus window driving through Rome, every shop, restaurant, and cafe was draped in red-white-and-green Italian flags, blue Italian National Team banners, and posters of players. Men, children, women—there didn't seem to be anyone in that country who wasn't caught up in the passion. Piazzas were filled with supporters singing and chanting, or sitting on their Vespas reading *La Gazzetta dello Sport* to make sure they hadn't missed any vital piece of information as their beloved "Azzurri" prepared to take on the Americans. The downside was that we were only in Rome for two days. But everyone we encountered during those 48 hours was happy to have us there and made us feel at home. Their passion for soccer drives grown men to tears, but rarely results in violence. The atmosphere was everything I could have ever wanted from a World Cup.

Going into the game, we had no idea what to expect from Italy. We were beyond nervous. After the hammering we received from Czechoslovakia, the papers were predicting scores anywhere from 5–0 to 10–0. Actually, after losing so badly in the first game, you would have thought that the whole team would be thinking that we were going to get slaughtered. But the Czech loss had only made us angry. We were a laughingstock. "The U.S. is terrible . . . The United States has no right to be here. . . ." We were dying to play again, work harder, play better, and prove that we'd earned our spot in the tournament, just like everyone else.

We knew we had to give everything we had. Baresi, Vialli, Donadoni—we knew their players and had seen them play. The only question was, did we know how to compete with them? The bus ride on the way to the stadium was tense and quiet. It seemed to take forever. You could see in the players' eyes that we were ready. The closer we got to the Stadio Olimpico, the more blue we saw and the more our adrenaline kicked in. Just as our bus was about to enter the stadium and the police were parting the crowd, I saw my parents, Cindi, her family, and all the other U.S. families and friends standing in the middle of the insanity, waving and cheering. It was exactly what we needed to see before disappearing under the stadium. As we drove through the doors and down the ramp, the sound of the crowd outside died down. But even though the doors were shut and we were parked below field level, we could hear the shouts and the songs in the stadium, and there were two hours until game time. It was electric.

Getting ready before the game, I was buzzing with anticipation—a high-energy buzz that I hadn't felt before any other match. The nervousness I'd experienced before the first game was gone and I just wanted to get myself organized before going out to warm up. I was talking to myself, taking mental notes. "Get your shin guards. Good. OK, now go get your legs rubbed . . . "As I got dressed and put my boots on, I had never paid so much attention to how I tied my laces. Everything had to be just right.

During warm-ups, I couldn't hear myself speak. I looked down toward the other end of the field and saw players I'd admired all my life. I was standing on the field looking around in awe and I noticed Tab trying to get my attention. He was only about 15 yards away and was obviously yelling, but I couldn't hear a word he was saying. When I got about two feet away from him, I could finally make out that he was saying, "Harkesy, is this incredible, or what?!!!" We were already in fifth gear and the game hadn't even started yet. Once the excruciating wait was over and the match started, we were on fire. We played at a level we didn't think we were capable of because of what it meant and how poorly our first match had gone. Playing in Rome's Stadio Olimpico before 80,000 was as exhilarating as it was intimidating.

Luckily for us, the Italians took us for granted after our pathetic show against the Czechs. They wrote us off, as if to say. "*Please*, the U.S.? We're going to kill them without even breaking a sweat." But by doing that, they gave us a lot of room to play, which helped build our confidence. We strung a few passes together and were able to move the ball around better than we had expected. I began to think that things might actually turn out all right, that a 5–0 loss was not in the cards. Ganz had given me the task of marking Roberto Donadoni, who I considered to be one of the best. He was such a quality player and I had tremendous respect for him, but I had to focus. Donadoni's running off the ball and his touch and vision made it hard to contain him. We had to work very hard to try to shut them down because they moved the ball so well. One thing I remember in particular is that they didn't say a word to us. No trash talking, nothing. Not one word. I'm sure the language barrier helped.

Early on, Italy was awarded a penalty shot, and I thought, "Here we go. We're going to get hammered." But Vialli stepped up to take the shot and he hit the post. We were still in the game. But it was only a matter of time before A.S. Roma legend Giuseppe Giannini, also known as "Il Principe," scored, and Italy went up 1–0.

We had our share of chances. Late in the game, Bruce Murray took a free kick that swerved around the wall of Italians, was blocked, and the rebound came out to Peter Vermes. Vermes cracked a good strike at goal from close range that bounced up between the legs of Italian keeper Walter Zenga and had him scrambling, but it was cleared away by one of the defenders. It would have been incredible to tie Italy in the World Cup. But the game ended, 1–0, and we had lost match #2. We were disappointed but not devastated, because we knew we'd played well. That match against Italy was the best game that particular U. S. team ever played, although I'm not sure what we'd think of our performance if we looked at the tape today.

And if we were disappointed, the Italians were embarrassed. They didn't destroy us the way everyone had expected, and the Italian press ripped into them because of it. The reaction that we got from the home crowd was total class. There we were, playing against Italy in Rome, and the Italian fans clapped us off the field. We'd walked into that stadium as the underdogs—again—and walked off with the respect of some of the most passionate and demanding fans in the world.

As we made our way down through the tunnel, all of us were trying to find players to exchange shirts with. I spotted Riccardo Ferri who wore number 6 and we swapped. A moment later, though, Giannini walked over and started motioning to me that he wanted to exchange jerseys. I pointed to my T-shirt as if to say, "Sorry, it's gone already." So he shrugged his shoulders and pointed to my shorts. Swapping shorts was a new one to me, but what was I going to say, "No?" So there I was, walking through the tunnel, shoes off, socks down around my ankles, casually strolling past the press in my T-shirt and underwear carrying someone else's shorts. I still have them: they're long and white with the Italian National Team "Calcio" badge on them. All of us as players were surprised that the Italians wanted souvenirs from *us*. And I thought, "Il Principe of the Italian National Team wants my shorts. It doesn't get any better than this."

Our third and last match was against Austria, a team we thought we could tie. With each game we had improved, and against Austria we created some good chances. But even though we played well, we lost 2–1. After the match, I was interviewed by the BBC. They asked me about my Scottish background, how I liked training with Sheffield Wednesday in January, and if I'd like to go back over there. I looked at the camera and said. "It was a great experience and I would love to have the opportunity to train there again." I hoped Ron Atkinson was watching.

The World Cup was over and I headed back to the States, but I didn't know what to do with myself. I rested. I went down to UVA and spent some time with my friends. It took a few weeks for me to process everything I'd gone through in the past several months. People forget that less than ten years ago we were practically nonexistent in the world of soccer. Our international success is almost taken for granted now, which is a sign of maturity, but back then we were breaking new ground.

I played a few games again with the Albany Capitals, but

I was basically back where I'd started: living at home in Kearny, hanging out, and playing soccer. I thought about the kind of future I could have in soccer in the States, and it didn't look good. I knew my choices at home were limited and I had to do something to keep myself sharp. The time left in my career for me to really "make it" was slipping away fast. I could see that without the World Cup or any real challenge on the field, I wasn't doing anything but biding—and wasting—my time. And after experiencing the European passion for soccer firsthand, the level of competition, and the challenge that it offered, I knew, somehow, I had to get back over there.

Standing on board the train from London to Sheffield, I had no idea what to expect once I got to my destination. I had thought about playing overseas since I was a kid, and there were no real career options in the States. But deciding to go off into the great unknown wasn't easy, and I doubted English football would welcome me with open arms. Somehow, though, I had to make it work. If nothing else, I at least had to know for myself whether or not I could make it.

No American player had yet succeeded in England, so I had no one with any real experience to turn to for advice. I made up my mind to go with the help of friends and people I trusted. I called Cindi and told her that I was thinking about going, and that this time, hopefully, it would be on a more permanent basis. Over the phone, she seemed to think it was a good idea, but I think she would agree that she didn't really grasp what I was venturing into and what kind of world I was going to be a part of: the cultural challenges, the competition, the setbacks. All the ups and downs that would come my way. Of course, I didn't either. She came up to Kearny and we had a long talk. In my mind I would be going over there for a year, two at the most. If everything went well, I'd make some money, gain valuable experience, and then come back to the States. My U.K. passport, possible through my parents, meant that I would be considered what they called an "assimilated player," not a foreigner, and that meant less hassle for any interested club. Cindi supported me, and so did my parents and friends in Kearny. Everyone seemed to agree that if I really wanted to make it as a player I had to give it a shot.

Ian St. John, Sr.—a big-time player who had turned agent—arranged for me to train with Sheffield Wednesday again. Sheffield manager Ron Atkinson, who had been one of the TV announcers for the ITV during the World Cup in 1990, said that he'd watched me pretty closely during the tournament and was willing to give me another look. My foot was finally in the door, but it was an American foot, and I was nervous as hell. Although I was 23 years old, in terms of professional experience, I was more like an 18-year-old kid. And I soon discovered that any apprehensions I had about being in England were well-founded.

Ian St. John had a management agency and he brought me over and started showing me around. But it was really his son, Ian St. John, Jr., who looked after me. At the time Ian was assigned to work with me, he was around 27, just a few years older than I was. We hit it off right away and it was a big relief to have a friend over there. Among other things, Ian made sure the club treated me well and had talks with Atkinson about my training.

After about a week, there were a few "hellos" here and there, but I was still on my own most of the time. The players weren't mean, just kind of indifferent, and I had no idea where I stood with them. I kept reminding myself that I had just played in a World Cup and had nothing to lose. I spent most of my time alone, in my small room in the Hallam Towers Hotel, a residence I would come to know too well. After about two weeks, some players started to open up and I began to feel accepted. But I somehow felt that guys made an effort to get to know me as a favor, taking turns looking after the young American lad. It was as though someone was saying, "Hey—take the kid out to lunch and sort him out. He's on his own."

I realize now that during my trial with Wednesday, Ron Atkinson wasn't only concerned about my physical abilities as a player. He was also trying to decide if I had the mental toughness to make it over there. He was worried, even if I proved to him I could play, that after four or five months I would want to go home. Taking on an American was a risky thing for Atkinson to do, especially if I didn't perform for him and for the club. I knew I could train for him as hard as he wanted, all day every day if he asked me to, because that's all I wanted to do. But surviving the loneliness, the culture shock, and the bias against American soccer players was not going to be easy. Atkinson didn't want to waste his time or his money on someone who was going to back out on him. So I was trying to prove to him that I was strong enough. And I had to prove it to myself, too.

I was training really well, and after about four weeks, Atkinson offered me a contract. Ian said, "Well, you got your foot in the door, Harkesy. I know it's not a lot of money." It wasn't, really. I was expecting more and so was Ian. Now, don't get me wrong, it was *good* money, about 650 pounds a week plus bonuses. Back then, that was comparable to about $1,000 a week or $4,000 a month. I wasn't going to get a salary like that playing in the States, and I certainly wouldn't get the same experience. In Albany, playing with the Capitals, I was getting around $400 or $500 a game—when the checks didn't bounce. Ian St. John, Jr. and I talked about it for a while, and he said, "You know, I could make a few calls if you want to check out some other clubs. I think you have the ability if you want to give it a go."

It was actually quite common for a player to try out with more than one club, so I said yes and the calls were made. I turned down the Sheffield contract, packed up all my gear, and headed to Blackburn to train with the Rovers. And when I did that to Ron Atkinson, I put him off. I know that now, and I should have known it then. He'd given me the chance to come back to train with his club and the chance to be a permanent part of the team, and I said "No." But Ian wanted me to test the market, and I trusted his advice. Although we knew the decision was risky, we thought being offered a contract at Sheffield would be good leverage at another club.

Ian was living in Liverpool and said he would meet me in Blackburn. I headed to the train station, hauling three or four loaded duffel bags with me, but there weren't any empty seats anywhere. I stood for the entire three-hour trip to Blackburn, surrounded by my luggage and looking like a tourist. That was when I started to second-guess my decision. Why didn't I just sign the contract back in Sheffield? All the way to Blackburn, I had nothing better to do but drive myself nuts and it didn't take long before I started to think that maybe I'd screwed things up. Gazing out the window of the train, I was certain I'd blown it. But then I told myself that I would make it work in Blackburn. I had to.

Back in 1990, Blackburn Rovers wasn't the club that they are now, mostly because they didn't have that much money. Ex-Scottish goalkeeper Don McKay was the manager at the time. I trained with them for a week and did fairly well, and McKay decided to offer me a deal—the same deal that Sheffield had offered me. The problem was that I knew Sheffield Wednesday was a better club than Blackburn, with better resources and a better coach. I knew then that I wanted to go back and sign with Sheffield Wednesday. So Ian called down to Sheffield and, before he could get a word out, Atkinson told him that the contract was off the table. It had become null and void the minute I'd stepped onto the train to go to Blackburn. At that point, I had no doubt that I'd wasted my one, good chance to play with a decent English club and I started to lose it. Regret, panic, despair—you name it. I was staying at a hotel in Preston, which is just outside Blackburn, and I was lonely, on my own, and all my fears and insecurities were being confirmed. I was convinced that my grand plan to be a professional in England would never work out, and that the only thing that made sense was to pack up and head home.

I called my mom and dad back in Jersey and told them everything that had happened. My father knew the game overseas and he knew what making it abroad meant to me. But he told me, "If you don't think it's right, son, come back home. I'm proud of you anyway, for what you've done." He told me that he thought I could make it if I wanted to. "I think you can stick it out, son," he said. But he didn't say that I *should* stick it out. After that call I felt better, but I still didn't know what to do.

The one phone call that finally convinced me to stay was the call I made to Cindi. I rang her at school and once I started to tell her about everything that had been happening I started to cry. I didn't feel comfortable crying over the phone to my girlfriend, but I couldn't help it. Cindi gave me a kick in the ass, believed in me when I'd given up on myself, and simply said, "John, you can do it. Hang in there and show them what you can do. This is what you've always wanted." That was a big turning point for me.

I look at Cindi sometimes and wonder what made her say that to me. I knew it was hard for her, dating me even though I was never there. I'm sure she never imagined that I would end up over there for six years. At that point I didn't think I'd be over there for another six days. But she gave me the strength to stay, and soon after that phone call, Celtic of Scotland contacted Ian St. John, Jr. and asked about my availability.

Billy McNeill was the manager of Celtic at the time and was the same man who had taken the Celtic youth teams over to Kearny to play games against the Thistle when I was growing up. Of course, my father is a Rangers supporter so I wasn't too quick to mention my trial with Celtic to him!

McNeill told Ian, "Bring John up to Celtic for a week—I'll sort him out." And I was off again. I packed my bags and headed for the nearest train station feeling a bit like a gypsy. I told myself what a quality club Celtic was and how incredible it would be to be a part of that organization. But more than anything I thought, "This is going to save me."

It was a five-hour train ride to Scotland, and by the time I arrived I was exhausted. The next day I was training like a madman, busting my ass, running all over the place. I was wiped out. Of course, it wasn't like I could strut up to the coach and say, "Uh, excuse me, coach, I'm a little tired from my five-hour train ride, would you mind terribly if I just warmed up today?" Not an option. The last thing I wanted to do was look weak. There's a lot of room in the States for the free-spirited player, but in Scotland and England there's not—none at all. You fall in line and do what's asked of you: nothing more and definitely nothing less. I had to do what they wanted me to do, in the way that they wanted me to do it, without questioning anything.

I ended up playing three friendly games for Celtic. The club had arranged a scrimmage for me and there were also two reserve games. So I played Monday, Wednesday, and Friday, three games, a full 90 minutes each, running at a hard pace. I did quite well, scoring twice. And during that week the support for me was much more than I expected. The papers were even writing articles about me. Outside the stadium, vendors were selling American flags—only the stripes were orange and the stars had been replaced by shamrocks. I felt like I was in—I had finally landed right where I belonged. At the end of the week, Ian St. John told me that it looked like the deal was going to happen. "You're going to sign a good deal. I think McNeill's going to double the wages you were on at Sheffield Wednesday and put you up. We might even be able to get you a club-sponsored car."

On Saturday, I went to watch the first team's match. It was a beautiful day, I'd had a fantastic week, and I was in my glory. I turned around and two rows behind me, in the director's box, was Kenny Dalglish, one of the best managers and players of all time. The crowd never stopped chanting. Sitting there in the massive atmosphere of Celtic Park, I couldn't believe that it was finally happening for me. I was getting a good look at the big time, and I had to be a part of it. I was thrilled that things were going well, but I started to get nervous, too. If I signed a contract, could I really do what needed to be done for the club? I sat there in the stands and watched different players and what they were doing on the field, the runs and the tackles that they made, their work rate. I wondered if I could play in front of a crowd that demanding and devoted week in and week out. But the game, the atmosphere, the flags, the songs—it was brilliant. It blew me away and I stopped worrying.

I stopped worrying a bit too soon.

Celtic had a nightmare game and Billy McNeill was on his way out. I went over to Celtic's clubhouse as soon as I found out, and someone in the front office who I had never seen before told me that *all* deals were off. I was under the impression that everything had already been settled and I refused to believe him. I refused to believe that I had gotten as far as I had just to have everything pulled right out from under me. Ian walked up and I explained to him what was happening. He told me to get back to the hotel and stay there until he rang.

In the cab on the way back to the hotel, I tried to stay calm. I told myself over and over that Ian would find a way to set things right. There must have been some kind of misunderstanding. But when I arrived at the hotel and went up to my room, two hotel employees were already there, and they weren't members of the cleaning staff. They were packing all my stuff. Packing my stuff *for* me, all my private gear. My clothes, my toiletries, my letters—they were randomly throwing everything I had into boxes and tossing them into the hall. I suddenly realized that I was being kicked out of my hotel room.

Ian came to meet me at the hotel, saw what was going on, and went completely berserk. He started grabbing things right out of their hands in a rage, yelling, "What kind of treatment is this?" I knew what kind of treatment it was: I was a "project" Billy McNeill had taken on, a Yank of all things, and the new regime was not going to have anything to do with me. I stood there and watched Ian argue with the hotel staff, unable to do anything while my life fell apart in front of me. One minute we were talking cars and contracts with Billy McNeill, and the next, total strangers were packing my toothpaste in with my socks.

I was trying to be polite, especially since I was an American and still felt like a guest in their country. So I said, as calmly as I could, "Can you put that down, *please*?" But they told me they had received specific orders from Celtic to "help" me get packed and to clear the room out immediately. Celtic would not be paying rent for the room anymore and it had to be vacated. By that time, Ian St. John was on the phone to Celtic, and it was clear from the tone of his voice and what was being said that he wasn't making much progress. I started to get angry myself, and demanded that the hotel employees get out. I was really pissed off and felt completely humiliated.

I repacked all my gear in a daze and dragged it with me to a nearby restaurant. Ian and I sat there for an hour or two while he made calls and I tried to figure out what I was going to do. I had a cup of tea—I felt too sick to eat—and called my relatives, my cousins, and my friends. I tried to explain to my friends living in Scotland what had happened without telling them the whole story. At first, all I said was, "I think I'm off again. It's not working out here." They were shocked because I was playing well and people were talking about me. I didn't have the guts to tell them what had happened at the hotel, because I was so furious and embarrassed. They kept asking for more information, so I had to explain that Billy McNeill had been fired and all deals were off. What made matters worse was that they were loyal Celtic supporters. So once I finally managed to admit everything to them, including the hotel fiasco, the story made them angry with their own club. That showed me what true friends they were, and at that moment, I needed friends more than anything because I felt like crawling under a rock.

Meanwhile, one of the calls Ian made while we were in the restaurant was to Ron Atkinson. To this day I don't know what he said to the man, but somehow he convinced Ron to let me have another chance with Sheffield. By the time the Sheffield news had sunk in—and I wasn't even sure what it meant yet—Ian had already bought me a train ticket and shoved me in a cab saying, "Get down there as soon as you can." There was apparently a reserve match the next day that I might be able to get in on, and Ian was going on ahead of me to sort things out with Atkinson before I arrived. But before

Ian drove off to try and mend my crumbling career, he said that the best—and only—advice he could give me was to work my butt off to prove to Atkinson, the directors, and the other players that I really wanted to make it in Sheffield. I'll always remember the way Ian kept his cool and calmed me down. He went far beyond the agent's call of duty. He said to me, "Harkesy, you're the one who makes it happen. Don't let anybody tell you different. I just do the paperwork. What you do on the field in training, what you do in the game . . . that's what's going to make it happen—not anything that I say." Well, something he said had gotten me another chance and I was thankful for that. I threw my newly reorganized stuff on the train and headed that night back down to Sheffield. The train was packed yet again and I stood the entire five hours. It seemed like a fitting end to one of the worst days of my life.

Another long train ride, another opportunity to stand in the corridor with my bags and wonder what the hell I was doing with my life. I was definitely at an all-time low. Five hours to think about why I'd left Sheffield in the first place, five hours to question whether or not I'd ever make anything of myself in England. But for the most part I was thinking that I was going right back where I started—back to Sheffield and the Hallam Towers. Only this time I was going back to Ron Atkinson with my tail between my legs, having had the most degrading experience of my life. The way things had gone from bad to worse—my post-Blackburn phone call to Cindi looked like the good ol' days at that point—I couldn't help but wonder if there was more disappointment to come. One thing was certain: I was going to have to earn that contract. Or die trying.

When I saw Atkinson again he gave me a knowing look that seemed to say, "See, I told you so. I knew you would be back here." I didn't know if he really was thinking that, but if he was, who could blame him? In training, around the clubhouse, and in every conversation I had with him, the look he had on his face let me know: "Now you've got to prove yourself to me all over again, son."

Everybody was winding me up—Atkinson, the players,

the front office staff. I was expecting it, and I did have it coming, so I took it. But despite the mistakes I had made, I think
Ron liked me. I think he understood me, too. Looking back, I
think he recognized that I was dedicated and he thought I had
the ability—on and off the field—to make it. Of course, at the
time I was just hoping to keep hold of my hotel room and get
in a few reserve games. I couldn't believe that I had already
passed up a contract with Sheffield and was having to go
through the whole routine all over again. But that's the way it
goes. No one was going to hand anything to me, especially not
after what had happened. I trained with the team and played
scrimmages and reserve games for a couple of weeks.

It was demanding soccer over there as a midfielder on the
wing, taking on players and getting the ball into the box. I certainly learned how to swing in a hard cross—the forwards always seemed to be there waiting for it—and I was getting on
the back post. I started to get close to some of the players and,
most importantly, I was actually scoring goals again—a lot of
them. And I knew that would help my chances considerably. I
was feeling better about my situation and things seemed to be
turning around. But after walking away from a contract, I
knew I had to keep showing that I was willing to do the work,
get "stuck in," and play their game. I couldn't let up until I
had a contract in my hand or was told to get on a plane.

Back in the States, a lot of international games were being
scheduled for the National Team. Sunil Gulati called me to
find out what was going on because Coach Gansler wanted to
call me in for an international friendly against Poland scheduled in Warsaw on October 10. At that time in the National
Team program, and at that stage in my career, I knew it was
very important to represent my country and be with the
team, and I wanted every cap I could get. The problem was,
there was a reserve match for Sheffield the same night. Sunil
must have been wondering how I could think that a reserve
match was more important than the National Team, but if he
was, he hid it well. He just asked me what I thought about
the situation and I told him: I had been traveling with the
first team again, and I was playing well and starting to feel

*Pictured here with Nigel Pearson, captain of Sheffield Wednesday,
doing an advertising campaign for phone cards.*

settled. I explained that the game was a big one—we were
playing Leeds United—and I thought if I played well I might
have a contract. Sunil told me to do what I needed to do,
wished me luck, and said that he would talk to Gansler and
let him know what was happening.

The night we traveled up to Leeds for the game I felt terrible. I was exhausted and starting to get rundown. During the
bus ride on the way there, I laid down on the bed at the back of
the bus, rested, and thought about the game. Fortunately, as
soon as the match started, I felt better. By that time, people
knew about me, who I was and, more importantly, where I was
from. I was getting my share of shouts, but nothing too out of
the ordinary: "Go home, Yank! Go play baseball!" I had started
to get used to it because I heard it all the time, and everybody
got taunted. It was part of the game and the tradition—and it
was half the fun. But when people jeer at me and wind me up

75

it just makes me want to play harder. And that night, those insults were exactly what I needed. We won 3–2, and I scored two of the goals. The next day, Sheffield offered me a three-year contract. At last.

Before I could sign, though, the club had to buy me from U.S. Soccer—something that was unusual—because I was still under contract with the Federation and it owned my rights. In most countries, clubs negotiate with clubs, not a country's national governing body for soccer. Sheffield ended up buying me for an amount in the neighborhood of 75,000 pounds, a bargain-basement deal. I was offered the exact same wages that had been offered to me months earlier, but there were some bonus incentives added into the contract. At that stage, after Blackburn and my disaster at Celtic, I just wanted to get my signature at the bottom of that piece of paper as quickly as possible. What an incredible feeling that was, not only to sign a contract finally, but to know that Atkinson had enough confidence in me to want me at his club for at least three years.

But that didn't mean things got any easier. Once I signed, the real work began. I had to break into the first team, and that meant I had to be mentally strong. But I've never wanted anything more. I became one of the top reserves, and Atkinson started taking me along on away games with the first team. I was traveling with them, training with them, and it gave me an opportunity to get to know some of the more experienced players. I knew there was a lot I could learn from them. Of course, the guys were still winding me up. But I grew up in that kind of environment and had traded sarcastic jabs with the best of them. I knew the Sheffield boys were waiting for me to get flustered and upset, so they could say, "Oh, poor Yank . . . He doesn't know how to take a joke." But everything there was said with a wink so I never took it personally. I enjoyed it and, more importantly, I gave it right back to them. And in that weird and wonderful English way, they appreciated it.

With every wisecrack that came my way, the more I felt like I belonged.

Some people think football is a matter of life or death.
I don't like that attitude. I can assure them
it's much more serious than that.

This quote is attributed to Bill Shankly, late manager of Liverpool. Good or bad, it gets repeated all the time, but that's probably because so many people from so many different cultures and backgrounds seem to agree with it. I know it has always reminded me of Sheffield, England, for a variety of reasons.

Sheffield is a steel town about 2½ hours north of London in Yorkshire, and the fans there were some of the best I've ever had the privilege of playing in front of. The town itself was, and still is, your basic blue-collar, working-class town, and it reminded me a lot of Kearny in that way. The people who lived in Sheffield thought it was small, but it's actually the fifth-largest city in England, and there was plenty of room for two teams to play there. The "other" team was Sheffield United and, because of their existence, the city is practically split right down the middle. It wouldn't be wise to live on the "United" side if you were playing for Wednesday—or vice versa. Some fans went as far as to paint their window sills blue and white to show their support for the Wednesday Owls. I had grown up in a soccer-crazed town, myself, but I had never experienced that kind of devotion from fans before.

Sheffield Wednesday, the club, was established in 1867,

making it the fifth oldest club in England. Like a lot of football teams, it developed out of a cricket club, and for a hundred years, supporters and their fathers and their grandfathers before them had gone to the grounds at Hillsborough to see Wednesday play. When you have that kind of history and that kind of following, the passion for the club gets passed down from generation to generation. The town of Sheffield had a love affair with their teams. Even people who were on the dole, or unemployment, set aside a substantial chunk of money to buy tickets. There aren't too many places in the world where ticket sales go up the season after a team has been relegated to a lower division, but that's exactly what happened in Sheffield after the 1989–1990 season, just before I arrived.

But that same season, Sheffield was the backdrop for a grim reminder that passion can be taken too far. On April 15, 1989, Sheffield's home field of Hillsborough was the sight of one of the worst disasters in sports history.

Liverpool was playing Nottingham Forest in an FA Cup semifinal match and Hillsborough was the neutral ground that had been chosen for the match. Fans without tickets were in the pubs long before kickoff, and eventually made their way over to the stadium to try and get into the terraces, which were standing room only. It was later learned that some members of the security force thought the kickoff should be postponed because the number of fans in the terrace pens was beyond control, but the game began as scheduled. The crowd kept pushing forward, and when Peter Beardsley hit the crossbar for Liverpool, the surge that followed caused 96 people in the central pen to be crushed to death against the bars that enclosed the terraces. Afterward, the bodies were laid out on the field so that they could be identified—a sight that stunned and saddened the world. The whole country was in mourning. The sport that meant so much to the country had caused one of the greatest tragedies anyone could remember. The terraces were soon replaced by seating and the metal bars removed. And every year on April

15, flowers surround the stadium, reminding us that as much as we love soccer, it is only a game.

After everything I'd been through, I was happy to be back at Sheffield Wednesday. I was learning more about the game—and myself—on and off the field, every day. I'd finally started to make it onto the bench for the first team matches, which doesn't sound like much of a promotion, but it was a huge step for me at the time. My debut finally came away at Swindon, when I came on as an emergency replacement in a League Cup match.

My chance came when Roland Nilsson, our right back, injured his knee. Roland was a Swedish international, an outstanding player, and one of the first friends I'd made at Sheffield. He had also been a roommate of mine for a while. An injury to a player is the worst possible way to end up on the field, and I felt particularly bad that Roland's injury had given me this opportunity. So I wasn't able to get too excited about my first professional start for Wednesday.

I was playing right back, which didn't bother me at all in the system that Atkinson played. It allowed for a lot of overlapping, so I had some freedom to go forward and get into the attack as much as I could. I was loving it. I was starting to become more accepted by the English crowds, even though they were still a little guarded. It worked to my advantage that I had a high work rate, because they were big on that. That night, my Uncle William came up from Derby to see the game, and afterward he, Ian St. John, and I had a dinner celebration and opened a bottle of bubbly. Later that night I called my parents and Cindi to give them the good news.

Off the field, things were coming along slowly. I eventually moved out of the Hallam Towers and into a miniflat in a place called Mayfair Court—basically one room with a little eating area. It wasn't great, but it was a step up. I would head down to training in the morning, which was usually at around 10:30. The Sheffield Wednesday clubhouse at the training ground was adequate but nothing fancy, and its most important amenity was the tea room. Hard to believe, I know, but there's nothing like a nice cup of tea in the morning. England may be beautiful, but it's usually cold and damp, especially in the winter. We'd arrive at the clubhouse in the morning, get changed into our gear, and Annie would be there with tea and toast for us before we went out on the training pitch.

After training in the morning for two hours or so, I had the rest of the day off. Most of the guys on the team had their own things to do, and a lot of them were married. As I got to know my teammates better, players like Nigel Pearson and John Sheridan went out of their way to have me over for dinner now and again. But I usually had to rely on myself for entertainment and I was really lonely. A lot of my time was spent settling in and getting used to my new surroundings.

For a long time, I didn't even have a car. Paul Williams, who was on loan to Sheffield at the time, was staying at Mayfair Court, too, and every once in a while I would borrow his. I was lucky he let me, because I was still adjusting to the steering wheel—and the oncoming traffic—being on the wrong side. But having access to a car didn't change the fact that I'd get home at about 2:00 in the afternoon and have the rest of the day to myself. The solitude was driving me crazy. I would've given anything to be stuck in a hotel room again with Mike Windischmann, even if he was wearing his headphones and ignoring me. I was constantly on marathon phone calls to my friends, all over the States, one after the other. I'd work my way through the time zones and my phone bill was massive. I'd talk about games, training, the weather—*anything*, and when I'd look up at the clock, three hours had gone past. Life got a little better once I moved into a flat owned by my teammate Carlton Palmer, but I was still banging my head against the walls.

The only relief I had at the time was going out with the boys. The time that I got to spend with Sheffield Wednesday was probably the best three years of my career so far, and there is no doubt in my mind that the reason we were so successful on the field was because of the way we got along off the field.

In England, a town is often measured by its nightlife. "It's a good night out . . ." is a big compliment, and Sheffield was definitely a good night out. One thing that took some getting used to was that the pubs, even the big ones, closed at 11:00 P.M. So from there, people went to the nightclubs which stayed open until 2:00 A.M. The favorite among Wednesday players was Josephine's, and a group of us would go there a couple times a month.

Josephine's is where I met Shaun Walker. Shaun worked the door at the club and meeting him was one of the best things that happened to me while I was in Sheffield. We hit it off right away and became close friends. We spent a lot of time together playing snooker, going to dinner, or watching games, and it was good to finally have a friend who didn't "work" with me. He also introduced me to his brother, Joe, and the rest of his family. Joe and Shaun's dad, George, had actually followed Sheffield United for a long time. But they lived right up the road from Wednesday's grounds and once I started to get them tickets for matches, they became regulars. George never went, but he always supported me. It was good to finally have some familiar faces in the stands. Shaun was my age and living with his parents. Joe was a bit older and worked for a major brewery delivering bitter. They were honest, down-to-earth, hardworking people and they opened up Sheffield to me. As much as I liked being with my teammates, I didn't want to spend all my time hanging around with footballers. I considered them good friends and enjoyed being with them, but the notoriety of being a player often brought around a lot of groupies, which I wasn't into. Spending time outside the soccer world also gave me a different perspective on life in England. I wanted to meet people outside the game, but it wasn't easy. The Walkers were true friends. They didn't care at all that I was a footballer, and that was important to me. You had to be careful there, like you would have to be in the States if you played basketball or football. It was hard to know who to trust. But the Walkers were always very genuine and I was lucky that I met them.

There was usually a line at Josephine's, but we rarely had to wait in it. Shaun and Joe were always there, along with the usual Wednesday guys: John Sheridan, Carlton Palmer, and David Hirst. Phil King would come along, too, when we could get him out. A lot of the guys were married, and if they couldn't come out clubbing, they would still go for a pint at Hanrahan's after a game or training. Those boys were unbelievable. They could drink and drink and drink, and the next day go out and train, no problem.

If a player didn't show up to the pub, we'd give them stick the whole day. "What's wrong? Wife's got a lock on you, eh?" Every player's response, because of the more traditional culture over there, was usually something along the lines of, "Oh no. I'm man of the house." I'd just laugh to myself. Those were good times, the kinds of moments I really miss. The playing was incredible and the atmosphere at the games was unbelievable, but the camaraderie—the way we all got along—that was impossible to replace.

Of course, there were also the pranks. Nigel Pearson was a master prankster. Kingy and Sheridan, too. They spared no one. But when I first arrived, I was on the receiving end of more than my share.

Most of the clubhouses in England have huge baths, about 10 ft. long by 5 ft. wide and 5 ft. deep. After games or practice, everyone would jump in because the English season runs through winter and the water was warm. The first day I witnessed this, the guys were sitting around in the baths, soaking, and they were covered with dirt. The water looked like a cesspool. I took one look at the dingy water and started heading to the showers. But they all started yelling after me, "Ahhh get in the bath, you tosser!" So, naturally, they dragged me out of the shower and threw me in. The next day when I walked into the dressing room after training, all my gear was floating in the bath—boots, shin guards, socks, everything.

There were other times when I would go to get dressed after training and my socks would have been cut so that my toes came out the end. Or when I was running late, I'd rush into the locker room to get ready and Pearson or Sheridan would have hidden one of my socks. I'd have to go out to training in street socks and Atkinson would scream, "Where's your kit? Whose socks are those? You're not stepping on this field like that—that's a fine." And then Atkinson would turn to give the rest of the boys a wink and have a chuckle himself. The senior pros were always giving out stick. I had gotten this kind of treatment from one level to the next, and although it intimidated some players, I was used to it. I could dish it out as well as I could take it.

When it came time for me to move out of Carlton's place, Joe Walker was moving into a new flat with his wife, Barbara, and they offered to take me in as a boarder. I said I'd stay a week or two while I looked for another place, but that turned into six months. They made me feel so at home—Barbara completely spoiled me—and I didn't want to budge.

Sundays were my favorite. In the morning, Barbara would make a full English breakfast, or "the full monty," as it was called, a phrase that's gotten a lot of publicity since the movie of the same name was made in Sheffield. Just like the movie, the "full monty" meant everything—in this case, cooked tomatoes, mushrooms, sausage, eggs. After breakfast, Joe and I would catch the local pub teams playing, come home for Sunday "dinner" at around 2 P.M.—roast beef, Yorkshire pudding, veggies—and be on the couch in time for the "Match of the Day" at 3:00: a perfect day. Soccer was everywhere. You played it, went to games, watched it on TV, talked about it in the pub. I loved it.

Even though I was beginning to have some semblance of a life, I still missed Cindi and my friends, and I would spend hours at night lying at the bottom of the Walkers' stairs talking on the phone. My phone bills were still enormous, but thanks to the Walkers and the guys on the team, I was starting to enjoy myself and build a life in England.

Life on the field was improving, too. Ron Atkinson had been brought into Sheffield in 1989 and his first season there the Owls had been relegated to the second division. The 90–91 season was about getting promoted back up again. And once there was talk of the new "super league," which would come to be known as the Premier League, Ron wanted

Sheffield to be a part of it. "Big Ron," as everyone still refers to him, was quite a character, and he really took an interest in my game. That also meant he harped on me every day, all the time. He'd scream at me, "Come on, Harkesy, son! Let's go!" And as soon as I did something right, he'd just say, "Do it again." He was the type of guy who had the personality to pull off being a taskmaster in training and someone you could sit down and talk with once you were done. He used to get out on the training field with us—he was a big guy—and chase us up and down the pitch yelling, "Come on, I'm an old man! You lads should be keeping up with me!" I had a lot of respect for Atkinson. He didn't demand respect from his players; he didn't have to. In the way he ran his club and treated his players, he earned it. He'd say, "Harkesy, I'm going to get the best out of you, son." And that just made me want to play the best I possibly could for him.

I learned something new every day when I went out on the field. It was such a valuable experience for me. It's hard now that I'm older and more experienced, because I don't always recognize that I'm still learning. The potential to learn is always there, but the further along you get in your career, the more you have to look into things on your own. Sometimes, there is no one there to teach you and push you, especially if you end up with a coach who has less knowledge about the game or less experience than you—or worse, both. You have to find it within yourself to do the work—take yourself out with a ball, practice free kicks, work on your shooting. More responsibility rests with the player.

My first season went much better than I ever expected and by the end of it we were third in the league. My "goal of the year" in December's Derby League Cup match turned my career around and it also helped us get to the League Cup final, a huge accomplishment for a Division II team. And we had to get past teams like Coventry City and Chelsea to get there. But the legendary Manchester United was waiting for us in the final.

The final was in April. My first year in England, and I was going to play in a League Cup final in Wembley Stadium, one of the world's most famous soccer grounds. The entire trip was something I'll never forget. After arriving in London, we had a relaxed training in Hyde Park—jumping over bushes, chasing after squirrels. Howard Feggins, who played "American" football with the London Monarchs, came out to our training and threw a few passes to me for the television crews. I think he was impressed that I could use my hands. Atkinson even joined in, and the media loved the storyline–Americans playing their "football" in London.

Then later that night, two nights before we were to face Manchester United, Atkinson threw a 37th birthday bash for Trevor Francis at the Royal Lancaster Hotel, where our wives and girlfriends were staying, and then took us out for a dinner at his favorite Italian restaurant in Mayfair. Everyone was invited, and we all sat around big round tables, drinking wine, eating pasta, and enjoying our accomplishment. I was still wondering whether I was going to play in the match, because I had been struggling with the same stomach tear that I had before the '90 World Cup and my playing had been week-to-week. But I was thrilled I was getting the opportunity to play any part in the whole experience. It was enough just to be there.

I did my best to take it all in, because I knew it wasn't going to last long. Atkinson had done everything he could to create an atmosphere that made us realize how special it was just to be in the Cup final. In doing that, he took all the pressure off of us and placed it squarely on his own shoulders. We were huge underdogs, and nobody expected us to beat Manchester United, which was, and still is, one of the fiercest clubs in the world. Instead of being nervous and tense going into a big match at Wembley, we were relaxed. It was a celebration.

Of course, Atkinson worked our butts off in training the next day. We were pretty sharp, considering. A few of the guys were struggling, and I was thinking the American idea of pre-game abstinence wasn't too bad after all. For me, it was an adrenaline rush just to train, in London, for a League Cup final. And then Atkinson took me aside and told me that I would be starting. I was honored he had that kind of faith in me, and I hoped I would measure up. Ron was also starting me over Trevor Francis, who was an older and more experienced player. I was surprised—it was an honor for me to be selected over Trevor—and obviously thrilled, but I knew Trevor wasn't happy with the decision.

In training, Atkinson talked about United's strengths, and he was on top of us the whole time, barking, "Come on, lads! You've got to be sharp! You got Paul Ince tackling you. You got Bryan Robson making tackles, Harkesy, in the midfield. Are you going to play like that or are you going to be sharp? Come on, now!" Roland Nilsson, now recovered from his knee injury, worked with me on how we were going to shut down Lee Sharpe on the left wing.

The night before the game, we stayed at Bisham Abbey, an old English hotel near Westminster Abbey where the England team is usually based, and where all the clubs stay when they play at Wembley. Banners of all types hung on the walls—English clubs, international clubs, everybody. I sat up that night thinking about the game and what it would be like to play in a League Cup final in Wembley.

The day of the game I put on my track suit and headed out to the bus. It was about a 45-minute ride from the hotel to the stadium, and everyone was in a good mood—relaxed, reading magazines, and kidding around. Then, suddenly, there was a man with a microphone standing at the front of the bus telling jokes, and he wasn't one of our boys. It was Stan Boardman, a very well-known English comedian and friend of Atkinson's. At that point I was sure that I would never have another coach like Big Ron.

The clever things Atkinson would do went totally against the approach of most coaches. Few could come up with the idea of hiring a comedian to perform on the team bus, let alone actually follow through with it. I've played for coaches who, on the way to a game, would say, "I don't want to hear laughing in the back of the bus. You've got to be serious and focused," which is pretty condescending when you're speaking to adults. But Atkinson's attitude was, "You did all the hard work, and now it's time to go out, apply that, and enjoy yourself while you're at it. You know what you have to do." And that's how he got the best out of everybody. Stan Boardman's standup routine got us laughing and Ron got exactly what he wanted—someone on the bus to loosen up his boys.

I was sitting in the back of the bus with Danny Wilson, Shez, and Kingy, listening to Boardman's jokes, talking to Danny, and reading *Match* magazine. Every magazine and newspaper had coverage leading up to the match, and I was getting a lot of press as the first Yank to play in Wembley in a League Cup final. It was flattering, but I also knew the pressure was on. Suddenly, Boardman interrupted his routine and Danny nudged me and said, "Harkesy—here we go, son." I looked up from my magazine and out the window.

The bus had turned the corner and was heading down "Wembley Way," a long, straight drive leading up to the stadium that, by tradition, only team buses are allowed to drive down. But pedestrians are allowed, too, and the street was swarming with people. And just beyond the crowd I could see the Twin Towers of Wembley, soccer Mecca. As I looked down the street toward the stadium, all I could see was the blue and white of the Sheffield Wednesday supporters, and only a glimpse of Manchester United red here and there. Blue-and-white jerseys, blue-and-white flags, blue-and-white hair—the turnout was astounding. As our bus got closer to Wembley, it parted the sea of people, all bouncing, chanting, and cheering us on, some of them bowing to the bus as we made our way through.

I was standing up now, staring out the window, mesmerized, and Danny said, "Take it all in, Harkesy, it goes really quick. You're a lucky boy, you know that?" Without turning away, I answered, "Yeah, I do realize it," and gazed at the sight in amazement.

"No," Danny said, "I don't think you will until a couple of years from now. Then you'll understand. Not many footballers ever get to go to Wembley, never mind in the first seven months of their professional career."

But Stan Boardman said it best to all of us there, "You can't let this lot down. They want to see you with the Cup."

And as he said that, I felt a huge rush of adrenaline. I wanted to jump off the bus and run straight out onto the pitch as soon as we stopped. Unfortunately, we had another two hours before the start of the match.

Driving into the stadium was an experience, too. The bus entered through two enormous, old wooden doors, pulled up to the dressing rooms in the tunnel, and then the doors closed behind us. They were the biggest doors I'd ever seen, and I thought to myself, "Where are we going, to see the Wizard of Oz?"

Once inside the locker rooms, there was so much rushing around—players getting dressed and taped, going through prematch routines—that the only place I could find some peace and quiet was in the bathroom. I wanted to be by myself, settle down, and get focused. I told myself it was just another game and I had to go out and play. And I prayed for help to get me through.

We warmed up and got changed into our kits, and 12 minutes before it was time to head out to the field, a bell sounded in the dressing room to let the players know it was time to line up in the tunnel. Looking up the incline ahead of me, I could barely see the stadium. Standing next to the Manchester United players waiting to go out, I was trying to stay mentally ready for the game. But I could hear all the emotion and passion of the supporters coming down from the stands and pouring onto the field. I've walked out of a lot of tunnels in my life, but nothing could have prepared me for that 50-yard stretch.

As soon as the crowd got sight of the teams, the noise was deafening. The Sheffield supporters were bouncing up and down, singing, *"Atkinson's Barmy Army! Atkinson's Barmy Army!"* Their voices mixed in with those of the Man U. supporters, who were singing their own songs, and the stadium was buzzing as we walked out onto the pitch and stood across midfield. There, it's tradition for a member of the royal family to come out and be introduced by the captains to every member of each team. We felt gypped that year because we only got a representative from Rumbelows, the sponsor of the League Cup—no Fergie or Di. But I was too nervous to care.

The whistle blew, we kicked off, and the crowd exploded. I was playing against guys like Bryan Robson, Gary Palister, Lee Sharpe, and Paul Ince. Players that I'd watched and admired, some of them for years. I looked at them and I was in awe, which is not a good thing when you're in the middle of a game. It felt a lot like when I was on the field with the Italians in the World Cup. Still feeling a little nervous, I kept reminding myself, "I have every right to be here, just like they do." I was playing right midfield and Roland Nilsson was in his position at right back, behind me. As expected, we were on the defensive to begin with. I caught myself looking at Ince when I was supposed to be doubling back and I had to tell myself that I had a job to do. "Don't screw up, Harkesy," was all I could think. It was a world showcase and I was in it as an American. I couldn't believe I was gracing the same field as those guys, at that stage in my career. But the more I got into the game, the more it was like any other important game. I had to be disciplined, but I needed to relax and enjoy myself, too.

The atmosphere inside the stadium never let up, not for one second. The supporters were yelling at each other, singing songs, chanting back and forth. But the Sheffield supporters had the run of the place, singing everything from old Wednesday standards to Monty Python's "Always Look on the Bright Side." When the Manchester United fans tried to rally their lads—and especially Mark Hughes—by singing, *"Hughes . . . eee, Hughes . . . eee,"* the blue-and-whites drowned them out with, *"Who's . . . eee, Who's . . . eee"* Down on the pitch, the constant ruckus was both thrilling and intimidating. Like Boardman told us: you can't let that lot down.

Paul Ince and I exchanged a few tackles. I respected all the players out there, but at the same time, I needed to show them what I was about. At one point, Ince caught me going across him, and tackled me from behind, nailing my Achilles. I jumped up on my feet and got in his face, to get the blood going a bit. I sort of lined up to him and he looked at me with a cocky grin and a wink and started taunting me. "Settle down! What ya doing out here anyway, ya Yank?!"

I started winding him up about his sizable forehead, and as he ran by I would put my hand to my own forehead, pull my hair back as far as I could, and call him "five-head." Ince came right back with a "Yankee" this and a "Hollywood" that. We challenged each other like this the whole game—the mind game within the physical game on the field.

The roughness of the match finally caught up with me when I got my nose cracked by Steve Bruce, a center back from Man U. We both went up for a head ball and down I went. The trainers said it was broken but it wasn't—just a bump, nothing too serious. Usually, no matter how serious it is, the trainer comes over to you with a bucket of water, squeezes a sponge on your head, and wipes your face down. By old English standards that was enough—you were then fit and ready to go back in for some more. I loved it: the "magic" sponge.

We were holding our own and were justly rewarded in the first half when Nigel Worthington took a free kick that was headed away—but not far enough—by Man U's Gary Pallister. Sheridan settled the ball, pinged it, and even though Les Sealey, the Man U. keeper, managed to get a hand on it, it went to the left of him and into the corner. Shez took off sprinting and we all ran after him. Our supporters were ecstatic—we weren't expected to be up one-nil versus Man U. It was complete pandemonium in the Wednesday seats. And those who weren't cheering sat there stunned.

I came off in the 87th minute for Lawrie Madden, an older player who was thinking about retiring and probably wouldn't play in another Wembley final. Atkinson wanted to get him on the field. It was class move, showing respect for a senior pro. I was totally exhausted from the intensity, physical and emotional, of the experience. We held on to beat Manchester United 1–0—a huge upset. It was indescribable—

to pull off that kind of upset in front of such a brilliant crowd that included Cindi, my family, and friends. Jim Byrnes, a friend from Kearny and huge sports fan (mainly baseball) who had attended a large number of major sports events, told me later that he had never seen another event like it.

The medal ceremony followed an age-old tradition. I had seen it many times on television, but now I was actually participating in it. The traditional procession led up the staircase to the medals box—the 39 steps, they call it—where the directors and the royals sat. As we walked up the steps, the fans nearby reached out to shake our hands and hug us, throwing down their scarves and hats for us to wear. We marched up in a line, behind team captain, Nigel Pearson. When the League Cup was handed to Nigel, he lifted it up and the crowd erupted. He got his winners medal, passed the cup back to the next player, and walked back down the stairs shaking everyone's hands. I watched the cup work its way back through the line and then it was finally my turn: David Hirst turned, handed the cup to me, and I launched it up above my head and the crowd gave me the same response that they had given the other players. I had it in my hands for maybe 15 seconds, but that was enough. Once I passed it on, I kept saying, "Thank you, thank you, thank you . . . " over and over to myself. I couldn't believe how lucky I was to have played in a World Cup and lifted the League Cup within a year's time. While we were taking our victory lap, a supporter threw me an American flag and I wore it around my neck. The papers used that photo repeatedly, but more importantly, that one gesture made me feel accepted for who I was and like an important part of what was going on. Sheffield Wednesday was taking home their first "silverware" in 56 years.

After getting showered, we went upstairs to the conference center where our families and friends were waiting for us. Nigel Pearson and Atkinson said a few things, and toasts were made. Then everyone headed back to the Royal Lancaster Hotel. On the bus on the way back it suddenly hit me, "Wait a minute—I just played in Wembley!" The whole in-

Taking it all in after winning the League Cup in Wembley.

credible, mind-blowing experience. It just went too fast for me.

That night there was a formal banquet set up for us at the Royal Lancaster. All the players were introduced and it was such an incredible honor to be part of that, to be called up on stage with my teammates. We were all still wearing the hats and scarves that the fans had thrown to us after the game, singing, *"Che sarà, sarà . . . Whatever will be, will be . . . !"* and all the other Sheffield songs. Phil King sang, "It's a praise for Sheffield Wednesday." Old Atky even gave us his version of "New York, New York." It was a great evening, and it went well into the wee hours of the morning.

We were free the next day and that was it. We had to head back to Sheffield and start training again because there were still regular season matches to play. We knew we had to fin-ish the season with enough points to move up to the top division so we put the celebration on hold and got back to work fighting for promotion. Ron gave us the discipline that was needed and we came together as a team and were willing to do whatever was necessary to reach our goal. And by the end of the season, we'd achieved what Atkinson wanted us to. We won promotion.

Within seven months, I had scored the ITV England goal of the year against Peter Shilton. I had won a League Cup Winner's Medal at Wembley. And I had helped Sheffield Wednesday win promotion. All the English players kept telling me, "You can quit now, Harkesy. You've done it all."

But it was only the beginning.

Maybe a little luck and good timing played a part in my success that first year in England—they usually do in life. But every time I was out on that field, playing against some of the best players in the world, I had to show them what I could do. Once I was off the field, I had to show that I was mentally strong enough to live in that atmosphere, under a microscope, every single day. And no matter how well I did, I was still an American, a Yank, and that meant that I had to be better and work harder than most of the guys on the field. At least it seemed that way. Today there's a huge influx of foreign players in England, but back then it was unheard of. I was taking someone else's job, an English player's job.

I was glad to come home for a visit after my first season in England. If I had been healthy, I would have gone right into training with the National Team and its new coach, Bora Milutinovic. But this summer, the doctors ordered me to rest and rehabilitate the torn stomach muscle that had been bothering me for more than a year. After about five weeks, I had to report to Sheffield for preseason training, but I knew that I would be back in the States soon because Sheffield was scheduled to play a few exhibition matches in the States as part of its preseason preparation. The highlight match was the game Sheffield played against the National Team at Veterans' Stadium in Philadelphia. Although there was pregame talk about my playing a half for each team, I ended up playing only for Sheffield—as honorary captain—in a 2–0 loss. After the game, I played tour guide and showed my English teammates—Viv Anderson, Danny Wilson, Shez, Carlton Palmer, and Hirsty—around. I felt obligated to show them the real New York, although I think they would've preferred limo service to the subway. Before we headed back to England, I proposed to Cindi and I was starting to finally feel settled.

When I went back to Sheffield for my second season the one significant change at the club was that Big Ron had left to take a job with Aston Villa and Trevor Francis went from player to player-manager.

The Atkinson move shocked the whole town. After such an incredible season, and after getting Sheffield promoted no one expected him to leave. He had even said in the papers that he would "have to be crackers to leave Sheffield now." The next thing the club knew, he was gone.

Everyone—players, staff, fans—was devastated. Ron had become a hero in Sheffield since his arrival two years earlier and fans feared a quick return to the mediocrity that had plagued the club for the previous five decades. So off he went to Aston Villa, where he lived, and in his place came Trevor Francis, who had played with me at Wednesday the year before. Trevor arrived in Sheffield from Queens Park Rangers, where he had been dismissed as player-manager reportedly after a player revolt. The first time I met Trevor, I was 11 years old and he was playing in the North American Soccer League for the Detroit Express. I thought it was odd how things had come full circle and, as an adult, I was now playing for him, the first-ever player to be transferred for a million pounds.

All coaches have different opinions and different ideas about how they want to run the show, and Trevor simply didn't look at me the way Ron Atkinson did. Despite the rumors, I didn't have any preconceived notions about Trevor as a manager. What concerned me most about the change was that I would have to prove myself all over again, after having earned a starting position the previous year. I was prepared to compete for any job, but at least at the beginning it didn't seem like Trevor was giving me a fair shot. It took me a good half-season to regain my starting position, even though I was training hard every day and played well when given the chance.

Fortunately, just as I was inserted into the starting lineup, the team went on a roll and ended up finishing third in the Premier League. It was an amazing finish for a club that had just been promoted, and it also qualified us to compete in the United European Football Association (UEFA) Cup, a major European tournament, during the next season. Playing in the UEFA Cup meant more games, better competition, great exposure, and a lot more money for the organization. I couldn't wait.

During the summer, the National team hosted and competed in the first-ever U.S. Cup. We won the tournament that year, defeating Ireland and Portugal, and tying Italy. The tie we earned against a traditional soccer power like Italy was, in a way, more of a thrill than the other two wins. Being an American playing soccer in England is a lot like the U.S. team competing internationally—there's always something to prove.

Cindi and I got married that summer and I was happy knowing that she would be coming back to England with me and that our long-distance relationship days were coming to an end. When we got back to Sheffield, Cindi and I found a house to rent not too far from the Walkers'. It was great to see the guys again, and we were all looking forward to the new season and the opportunity to play in Europe. Everyone was optimistic, not just because of our third-place finish the year before, but because Sheffield had signed Chris Waddle during the summer. It was a move that stamped the club as big-time and put us in position to make a run at the league championship.

If I had to name one player I admired the most, or the one who had the greatest influence on my life and my career, it would have to be Chris Waddle. He signed schoolboy forms with Coventry at 15, made his first appearance for Newcastle at 19, went on to play for Tottenham, and had an incredible career as part of the English National Team. He had also played in Marseilles and became a legend in France. When he decided to come back to England, he came back to play with Sheffield Wednesday.

Chris could run down the field with the ball glued to his boot, carrying players in his back pocket. And he had great vision. Any quality defender would tell you that one of the most frightening sights you could see in your career was Waddle tearing down the wing at you. I remembered watching him on old videos, when he first started out; a young kid at Newcastle. And I had the chance to watch him in the '90 World Cup. Too many people, when they think of Waddle and the World Cup, think about the penalty shot that he missed in the semifinals against West Germany, instead of everything else he contributed to that team and their success. At Sheffield, Chris completed what was already an incredible group of players. When I heard he was coming to play with us, I couldn't believe it. I hoped that I would get along with him. But that turned out to be easy.

The first day he was at the club, he struck up a conversation with me in the dressing room out of nowhere. Despite everything he'd accomplished, Chris was very down-to-earth. He was a lanky guy who played down his size—he was over six feet, but carried himself like he was 5'10"—kind of quiet, but very friendly, with a great sense of humor. We hit it off immediately. Chris and I had the same personalities off the field, listened to the same music, and had similar backgrounds. Eventually, we got Cindi and his wife, Lorna, together and the two of them got on great as well. For Cindi and me, the Waddles quickly became valued friends and still are today.

Chris also knew how to be a true professional. I wanted to be on the same level as he was, so I watched him and did what I could to learn from him. I was thrilled to be playing every day with one of the best players in the world, someone

I could learn from. As the season progressed, I got to know him better and better. It also meant a lot to me because soccer players over there have a hard time getting close to anyone. There are so many transfers, trades, and loans, players know they're probably not going to be around for long. There's socializing in the pubs, but most players keep their guard up. Chris did keep his cards pretty close to his chest, but he also became a true friend and valuable teacher.

He was on the right wing, a dominant left footer. I was on the left wing, a right footer. I'd study certain moves he'd make, how he'd take on players, the way he got off a shot. He helped me incorporate balance into my game: when to hold, when to pass, and how to make the right runs. He helped me with my movement off the ball in general, and with taking players on. All of these subtle things are still a big part of my game and Wads helped me develop them.

After games and training sessions, Chris would often spend time with me, one-on-one; he'd set up cones, we'd run at them as if they were players, doing different moves, and work on putting balls into the box. That was my job as a winger. To a certain degree, it's a different game in MLS. Some players on the wing don't get the ball in early enough. They cut back, keep possession, and knock the ball back around again. That's not wrong, but there needs to be a balance. In England, if you're on the wing, you have got to get the ball, beat your man, and get the ball into the box, because the forwards are expecting it. They're making runs, and if a forward doesn't get on the end of your ball, that's his fault. Chris helped me to whip the ball in to the back post and to cut back on my right to get a defender on his heels. That's when my game really started to improve.

There was more of a mentor system in England than there is here. The older players were respected and, if you were smart, you did everything that you could to learn from them. A lot of that had to do with history and tradition, but there was also a lot more discipline from early on. Anyone hoping to become a serious player started kicking a ball around from day one, and studying the trade seriously at 16, or sometimes even earlier. At that age, a kid can become an apprentice—shining boots, laying out the players' kits for them, and training with the apprentice team every day. Players are instructed and they learn according to an established system. It's a fight to get off the bench. There's so much competition for every spot, no one can ever take his position for granted. More importantly, the mentor system is not something that goes away once you go pro. And during my third season at Sheffield, I learned a lot.

Sheffield's 1992–1993 season turned out to be almost as good as expected. Although we didn't win the Premier League and got knocked out of the UEFA Cup relatively early (by the German club Kaiserslautern, Thomas Dooley's team at the time), we did make it to the finals of the FA Cup *and* the League Cup—unfortunately losing to Arsenal in both—and went to Wembley four times. Making it to both finals—especially the prestigious Football Association (FA) Cup, the oldest English tournament involving all divisions—in one year was no easy feat. In a short time, Sheffield had become one of the most respected teams in the league.

Although it's hard to compare the four matches, the most memorable trip to Wembley was probably the FA Cup semifinal we played against Sheffield United. The game was to be played on neutral ground so that neither team would have an advantage. The original plan was to play the match at Old Trafford, the Manchester United grounds, but the people of Sheffield—on both sides—fought to have it played at Wembley. Both teams were playing for bragging rights, and the day of the match, Sheffield turned into a ghost town. No one was on the street, and most of the shops were closed. There were 80,000 people at Wembley, and practically all of them had come down from Sheffield. Forty thousand were in blue and white, and 40,000 in red and white, dividing the stadium into two colorful—and very noisy—halves. When the teams walked out on the field, foghorns blared, firecrackers went off, and thousands of red, blue, and yellow balloons were released. Even senior pros were dumbstruck by the atmosphere and the intensity of the supporters. I got to start in the match, something that I never took for granted. And the only thing better than the atmosphere that day was winning.

It was Waddle's game. In the first minute, he had a blinder, scoring a rocket of a goal on a free kick from 30 yards out and we were suddenly up 1–0. But United equalized late in the first half and we would have to wait until the second period of extra time to settle the score. Two minutes in, I took a corner from the left that cleared the near post and found Mark Bright. He was unmarked and easily headed it into the net. The roar from our fans was deafening—it was hard to believe that half the stadium was against us. Nothing could compare to winning in front of an all-Sheffield crowd in the greatest stadium in the world. Now we were on our way to the FA Cup final. And I would be the first American ever to make the trip.

We got a warm-up for the FA Cup final against Arsenal when we first met them at Wembley for the Coca-Cola League Cup final. Nine minutes into that match I scored what was probably the second most important goal of my life, off a clearance from a set play. John Sheridan faked a shot, and instead cut the ball to Phil King down the wing. Kingy crossed it into the box and when it bounced out to me, I hammered it low into the net past David Seaman, the current English National Team goalkeeper. I immediately took off down the pitch, with Waddle in close pursuit, while up in the stands, my family and friends were yelling themselves hoarse and hugging complete strangers.

Suddenly, the crowd began chanting, "Ooh, aah, Johnny Harkes, say ooh, aah Johnny Harkes . . . " It was an incredible feeling—one I'll never forget. We ended up losing 2–1, which was disappointing, but I was proud to be the first American ever to score in a League Cup match at Wembley. In three seasons, I had one winner's cup medal, a goal in Wembley, a runner's-up cup medal, and I still had a chance to win the most prestigious cup in England.

Winning meant even more to Chris because he had no winner's medal from England. Even though he had won titles in France and played in the semifinals of the World Cup, winning a League Cup or FA Cup medal means everything to an English footballer. He was 34 and it was probably his last chance.

We tied the FA Cup final against Arsenal 1–1, which meant that a second game had to be played. We were tense going into the replay because we wanted to win so badly, whereas Arsenal was very relaxed because they already had one cup under their belt and felt certain their name would be on the FA Cup as well. As we lined up in the tunnel for the rematch, waiting to go out, I remember not wanting to say a word to any of the Arsenal guys. I looked down the line— Tony Adams, David Seaman, Ian Wright, and others—and as I did, Ian Wright suddenly turned to me and said, "All the best, Harkesy." I was pleasantly surprised, and said: "Cheers, Wrighty." Then he added, with this huge wiseass grin on his face, "A bit nervous, mate?"

"Not at all," I said, looking out to the field.

"Well then, I hope I'm not running the ball at you today," he said, trying to wind me up.

It was dark and rainy, and the soccer wasn't very pretty— the play was hectic, our timing was off, and elbows were flying. One of those elbows belonged to Sheffield's Mark Bright and when it found the nose of Arsenal's Andy Linighan blood went everywhere. But Linighan would not be so easily stopped. Thirty-three minutes in, Wrighty slipped one past our keeper, Chris Woods, and Arsenal was up 1–0. Wads leveled the score midway through the second half, and it would stay tied until the *last minute* of the second period of extra time. And just when it looked like we were destined for a penalty shoot-out, Andy Linighan—busted nose and all— headed the ball right through Woodsy's hands and we lost 2–1. We all collapsed to the ground. Less than one minute away from going to penalties and possibly carrying away the winners' trophy, and suddenly everything was over. There was just enough time to kick the ball off before the final whistle blew, and the Arsenal fans went nuts. Their team had won the double—not unheard of, but still pretty incredible. I sat on the ground holding my head in my hands. We hated letting down the supporters who had never given up on us, and we had nothing to show for all that we had worked for that season. I looked over at Wads and he was teary-eyed. Wrighty walked over, shook my hand, and said, "You done well, Harkesy. You should be proud of yourself."

Despite the role I played in both cup runs and the final matches themselves, Trevor was still not convinced that I could play regularly at this level. There weren't any big blowouts between us, but there was constant tension. I didn't have the same relationship with him that I'd had with Atkinson. No one did. I knew Trevor didn't respect me as a player and that infuriated me. I thought after playing under him for a couple years—not to mention scoring in the League Cup Final—that he would come around and negotiate my contract fairly.

I had to leave for the States soon after the FA Cup final to play with the National Team and I couldn't wait to get home. I loved playing and living in England, but I wanted to see my family and friends and catch up on what was going on. Unfortunately, being away made it hard to continue contract negotiations with the club, and my situation was unresolved when I got back. So going into what would have been my fourth season with Sheffield, I was still on my original and very mediocre contract that Atkinson offered me when I first arrived. I came back for preseason on a week-to-week contract, until Trevor and I had a chance to sit down and talk about my future. We met and Trevor said he wanted me to sign a new, four-year contract for an amount that was barely more than what I was then getting paid. I didn't want an extreme amount of money, but it had to be reasonable and Trevor wouldn't go anywhere near the amount I was looking for. He basically told me that the players he gave the big money to were English internationals—not American ones—which I obviously thought was a tad insulting. He never said anything specific to me about problems he had with me as a player. In fact, in the same meeting, he told me I'd played brilliantly in the past year, which frustrated me even more.

It was killing me because I loved Sheffield. I loved the

fans. I loved living there. I loved the players. I loved the football that we played. I remember the tiny American flag that one fan used to hang over the player's tunnel at Hillsborough for every home game and how it made me feel accepted there. I wish circumstances could have been different because I would probably still be there today.

Although I hoped I could work something out with Trevor, I thought I should start looking around just the same. Arthur Cox, the manager from Derby County—a Division I team at the time—found out about my situation at Sheffield through Waddle, and said he was interested in me. So Arthur talked to my agent at the time, Mel Stein, who also represented Chris, Paul Gascoigne, and other big-name players. Chris really came through for me, and spoke very highly on my behalf. Cox had a lot of respect for Waddle's opinion and soon put in an offer for me to Trevor.

I started to think that I didn't want to drop out of the Premier League right then. I couldn't see how dropping down to a Division I team would help my career. More importantly, I wondered how it would look back in the States only a year before the World Cup. I called back to the Federation and talked to Sunil Gulati about it. I also discussed it with my dad. And I talked to Chris, who said, "Look, I'll tell you straight up: this is a short career, you've got to look out for yourself. If it's a good deal and you think you can make things work for you on the field, you've got to do it."

The negotiations back and forth between Trevor and me were all over the papers even though, as far as I know, neither one of us was talking to the press. I was offered lots of money from various tabloids to dish some dirt on what was going on behind the scenes at Sheffield, because other players were having problems with him, too. Still, I didn't give the papers what they wanted. I wanted to make it work at Sheffield Wednesday, and kept hoping that Trevor would come around and give me a bit more salary. If he had budged even a little, I probably would have stayed.

In the meantime, I tried to go about my business training with the team, but Trevor was obviously done with me. To make things more difficult, I had been competing with Danny Wilson for a spot in midfield. Trevor was close friends with Danny, their wives were close, and when Danny started playing midfield, competing for my spot, Trevor didn't hide the fact that he preferred Danny to me. I hated not playing and it was driving me crazy. Friends on the team told me I was being blackballed—that was Trevor's way. He wanted me for cheap, and I'm sure he told the board that he thought I would eventually break. But I had proved I was good enough and I thought I should be paid accordingly.

Even though I was competing with Danny, I had to leave my frustrations at work and on the field. But at the same time, it was on my mind a lot. It was easy to be competitive with Danny, and I knew he could tell that I was angry and frustrated because it was coming out in training. But one night we went out after a game and Danny was mature enough to raise the issue. He suddenly said, "Look, Harkesy, I don't resent you and I don't expect you to resent me. It's nothing personal between us."

The comment caught me off guard because I didn't expect him to come out with it. But I was relieved too. I would have been more likely to continue to let it frustrate me and to act like nothing was happening. But that would have been a mistake, because every day in training that you *don't* talk about those frustrations, the anger on the inside comes out on the field and that doesn't solve anything. It's bad for the entire team. As soon as Danny brought the topic up, all the other players at the table looked at me. They were waiting to see how I would respond. But I said, "No, I don't resent you. I just think I should be starting. I'm angry."

"You should be," he said. "I respect you more for that. If you weren't angry, I'd think you weren't a real player."

That was that. I was still mad that I wasn't playing, but the air had been cleared. Ironically, Danny and I would both end up leaving Sheffield that year. But we would leave friends.

I was one of several guys who didn't know where they stood with Trevor. The team got together to talk about what we could possibly do as players and how we could make things work. The team didn't rebel against Trevor; no one wanted to lose what we had there. As a younger player, it was interesting for me to watch how the older guys took on the responsibility of keeping the team together. Looking back, I realize there were many similarities between the situation with Trevor in 1993 and the situation with National Team Coach Steve Sampson in 1998, although in the latter case I was one of the older guys trying to hold the team together.

I knew things were really over on team photo day. I was still a Sheffield Wednesday player, so I got dressed and started to walk out onto the field with the other players. I ran into Trevor standing at the top of the tunnel and he said, "No—you are not in this photo. You haven't signed anything, so as far as I'm concerned you're not a Wednesday player. Get back inside and get changed." Then he said the same to Peter Shirtliff, which shocked both Peter and me because Peter was a senior pro. I walked back into the dressing room, obviously upset. Carlton Palmer, Chris Waddle, and Chris Woods were there and they went into Trevor's office and argued on Peter's and my behalf. But Trevor was adamant and said, "If they haven't signed, they know where they stand. There's no possibility they're getting in that photo." Right then and there, I knew my time at Sheffield Wednesday was over. Trevor also wanted to buy Andy Sinton from Queens Park Rangers and getting rid of me would make that a lot easier.

Trevor originally wanted 1 million pounds for me, and Derby counter-offered with around half that. Since they couldn't come to an agreement, my transfer fee was set by the tribunal at 850,000 pounds—the first time an American player was valued at more than $1 million. I sat down with Mel Stein and then went to Derby, where I talked to Arthur Cox and met the people at the club. I came back up to Sheffield and, for a week or so, I had a chance to think about my choice and make up my mind.

Three days after I came back from Derby, Trevor called me at midnight saying that Peter Reid, manager of Manchester City, was interested in me and that he would call the next

110

morning. I thought it was very strange that Trevor would call me at midnight on behalf of another team, so I told him that Reid should call my agent. Trevor insisted that Reid wanted to speak to me directly. That sounded out of the ordinary to me, but I let it slide. At nine o'clock in the morning, I got a phone call from Peter Reid. Peter said a lot of nice things, all of which sounded genuine. As a player, you want to believe the good things you hear. And Manchester City was a major club, so I thought it could be the answer to my problems. But when I suggested to Peter that he talk to Mel Stein, he said he didn't work that way and insisted on dealing with me directly. Trevor called and told me not to bother to come into training.

The Andy Sinton deal had already gone through, so I was stuck between a rock and a hard place. There was no place for me in Sheffield; if I talked to Man City I'd blow it with Derby; and if the Manchester deal fell through, I'd be left with nothing. On top of all that, the fact that Peter Reid was very close friends with Trevor made the Man City deal sound very dodgy. I trusted and respected Arthur Cox, so I signed with Derby and was done with it.

One week later, Peter Reid was sacked as Man City manager.

Soon after I signed on with Derby County, Arthur Cox developed a slipped disk in his back, and he was struggling. Arthur had been the most appealing thing to me about Derby. I liked his honesty. He had top-notch experience and had coached players like Waddle, Gascoigne, and Kevin Keegan while they were still young, playing a large role in developing their talent. As it turned out, I only got to work with Arthur for two or three months and I was very disappointed. For a while, Arthur called in the team sheet from the hospital and had his assistant, Roy McFarland, run things. But it wasn't long before Roy took over as the senior coach and Cox was out of the picture. The end of three great years with Sheffield, all the controversy surrounding my trade to Derby, and now this.

Derby, the city, was very small and not much to look at,

but the outskirts were beautiful. The area was mostly farm-
land, and after a time Cindi and I bought a converted barn in
a small town called Duffield. I guess buying a place made me
feel a little more settled, which sounded like a good idea
being that it was, after all, my fourth year in England. Until
that point, we were still living in Sheffield, and I had to drive
up and down the M1, 45 minutes each way, to get to work. I
wasn't anxious to leave my friends in Sheffield, but at the
same time, I knew I needed to make a clean break. My Uncle
William and cousin Neil, who used to drive up to Sheffield
to see me play, lived in Derby and were happy to have me
playing for their home team. And I was glad to have them in
the stands.

My contract with Derby was a good one and the club was
very ambitious. They wanted to move up from Division I to
the Premiership and had spent nearly 12 million pounds on
players to try and make it happen. We played at the Old
Baseball Ground, a dilapidated reminder of a time when
some English folks thought baseball was worth playing. I still
missed the guys at Sheffield, but I soon made good friends
and spent most of my time hanging around with Darren Was-
sall, Gary Charles, and Tommy Johnson. When I first arrived
the guys went out of their way to make me feel like a part of
the club.

I had only been to training a few times when McFarland
decided to take us to a local park to run. I knew how to get to
Derby's grounds, but not to the park, so a few of the players
offered me a ride. On the way there, they decided to stop at a
gas station and get some candy. Everyone had crammed into
one car so we all had to get out. Unfortunately—and as
planned—I was the only one who didn't get back in. They
left me at the gas station and went on to training without me.

I started walking up the road and assumed I'd eventually
find my way to the park. Other players were flying past me,
honking, "*Beep-beep*!!! Haaarkesyyy!" It was their way of
telling me that I wasn't going to stroll into their club like
some big-timer. I was going to get treated just like everybody
else. It was all part of the process. If they didn't take the time

to "welcome" you, that meant you were nonexistent and they couldn't be bothered with you.

On the field we had our work cut out for us from the beginning. After the club spent so much money on players, there was a lot of pressure on us from management and fans to produce results. The fans were not quite as supportive as the Sheffield crowd and were bitter because Derby hadn't been topflight for a few years. Everyone was anxious for us to be back on form. The surroundings were much better, but the supporters were not. I had been spoiled by the fans in Sheffield. Every game was do or die, and it was a hard go in the beginning. But then we started playing very well, got on a run, and the fans started to come around, creating a much better atmosphere. We ended up making it to the Division I playoff finals, which would determine whether or not we got promoted. Along the way, however, we met Millwall, one of the toughest clubs in East London. The match was played at their grounds and it was total insanity.

Everyone in England is familiar with Millwall's reputation. Cindi went to the match with Cheryl and Pat Nelson, good friends of ours who we'd met through the Waddles. They lived in London and would not let her go to the Millwall match alone. Cindi was thankful to have them along. Later Cindi told me that on her way into the stadium, fans were saying things like, "There's going to be carnage tonight." Even though we'd been in England for a while, neither of us had really experienced England's infamous hooliganism up close.

Millwall's home field is in a rundown part of London and is called "The Lion's Den." That name is far too mild. We'd already beat them 2–0 at home in the first game of the home-and-away playoff, so we knew they would come after us. Their fans had started trouble when they came to Derby, but that was nothing compared to what was waiting for us in the Den. Before the match had even started, we noticed a car from Radio Derby had been overturned. These were angry people. You could feel it walking into the stadium. It was evil.

Kasey Keller, my teammate on the National Team, was in goal for Millwall then, before he moved to Leicester City. I talked to Kasey before the game, and he just said, laughing, "Good luck coming down here. I can't be held responsible for anything that happens at this club." While we were warming up, shouts were already coming down from the terraces. "Derby bastards!" was probably the most affectionate of the names that we were called. Then came the comments against our black players. The "Kick Racism Out of Football" program was already up and running in England, but there were still a lot of problems. I was shocked at the racism over there. I know that racism is a problem in the States, too, but it was so blatant and in-your-face at some games. I was stunned.

The game started, and we were all over them from the beginning. It was a very physical match, and the referee was letting a lot of things go. But we were playing well, and we got on the scoreboard first. Right after the first goal went in, 10 or 12 people from the crowd managed to get onto the field and started to run at us, but security managed to catch them before they got too far. I couldn't believe that they'd gotten anywhere *near* the field. Things got progressively more nasty and the tension was building inside the stadium—on the field, and definitely in the stands.

Throw-ins became a matter of life or death. I'd get the ball against the boards, and these animals would be hanging over the wall, screaming, "Come on, ya Yankee bastard! Come and get it! I'll tear y'apart!" There was no way I, or any of the players, would throw the ball in unless the ball boy retrieved it first. We held on, scored again, and it didn't look as if anyone had gotten onto the field. But shortly after the second goal, we had a goal kick. When I looked back at our keeper, he wasn't taking the goal kick, but he was running. I wondered what the heck was going on.

So I turned and looked back upfield, and there were people streaming onto the field from the other corner of the stadium, running at us, screaming obscenities. This was not a group of 10 or 12 like before, but more like 100 or so, headed

*Celebrating with Gordon Cowans after a goal against Millwall in
the 1st Division playoff semi-final. Kasey Keller is below me
on the ground.*

right toward us, and there was no way that a few security
guards were going to be able to do a damn thing about it.

The whole team sprinted off the field and into the tunnel,
which was fortunately at the middle of the field. Even so, the
police had to extend the tunnel entrance by forming two
lines and making themselves into a human wall. So right
there, in the middle of the match, the entire pitch was
cleared. We stood in the tunnel for 10 or 15 minutes and
waited for things to settle down. We could still hear the
screams outside as security tried to haul away as many people as they could and get things settled.

The English players were more used to this kind of thing
than I was, but even they were floored by the whole scene.
Paul Simpson and Tommy Johnson were saying, "This is
mad, Harkesy, mad! . . . But it's brilliant isn't it?" I couldn't
believe they were laughing about it.

I said, "Are you kidding me? Our lives are at stake here.
I'm not going back out there."

"Ahhh, but Harkesy, what are you talking about?" they

said stretching and trying to stay warm. "You got to go back out, son."

And I did have to. We all did.

When we got back out, the crowd started up loudly with the racial slurs, and the referee told us that we had better start making some substitutions. So we got all of the black players off the field because we knew, by the end of the game or even sooner, there were going to be some serious problems.

When we scored again and were up 3–0, another mob came onto the field.

This time the lunatics came up from behind me and they were gaining fast. They were right on my heels, swinging at me. I was dodging in and out of people and as I was about to get to the tunnel, I looked back and saw that our keeper, Martin Taylor, had been knocked down.

I knew somebody had to go help him. But at that point, if anyone close to the tunnel turned back, we were all done for. Luckily, Craig Short, our center back and one of the bigger players on the team, was near him. Craig picked Taylor up, and started swinging and shoving people out of the way as he made his way through the mob toward the tunnel. No one was laughing this time.

And we still had to go back out one last time to finish the game.

None of us really had the energy to go back out into the mayhem, and we were also worried about getting into the tunnel in one piece after the final whistle blew. There wasn't a lot of time left in the match so, before we went out, the referee told us to look at him whenever there was a goal kick. When we reached the 87th minute, he would wait for the opportunity to blow the final whistle as a goal kick was being taken. Then all we would have to do was run like hell straight off the field. And that's what we did. Lucky for us, there was a goal kick and the ref gave us the nod. As the kick was taken, the whole team sprinted across the field and he blew the final whistle before anyone figured out what was going on. Once we hit the tunnel in our studs, everybody started slipping and sliding all over the place, falling into each other and running into walls. Looking back, that part of it was kind of funny. Life-threatening, but funny.

Once we had a chance to catch our breath, we were able to enjoy the fact that we'd won 3–1, and would be going to the playoff finals. But then we realized: wait—how are we going to get out of the stadium?

I n the months leading up to the 1994 World
Cup, I stayed in touch with the National
Team by fax and talked to the guys when I
could. The team was playing a lot of friendlies, but I stayed
in Derby and missed almost all of them. The closer it got to
the World Cup, the closer to the breaking point the players
sounded. "Double sessions, Harkesy, every day double sessions. We're going crazy." But even though it sounded like
torture, I couldn't wait to get back. I could just see it—Derby
would get promoted and I'd get to play in my second World
Cup at home in my own country. Things would be ideal.

Well, that fantasy didn't last too long.

Derby lost to Leicester City in the playoff finals and, as a
result, we didn't get promoted. The town hated us, the club
wondered why they'd spent so much money on us, and I was
devastated. The day after the Leicester match, Cindi and I
packed in a daze, got on a plane, and flew to L.A. to join the
National Team. The start of the World Cup was only two
weeks away.

I was trying to pick myself up, but I wasn't ready for the
most important soccer tournament in the world. I was physically tired from the Derby season, which had lasted until
May 31, and emotionally I was a wreck. I needed to relax and

wind down. During the 10-hour flight to California, the entire Leicester match ran through my mind—the chances we had and the mistakes we made. I only had three days to be alone with Cindi before I had to report to the U.S. team and Coach Bora Milutinovic. Once I reported, I tried to get settled as quickly as possible and get my mind on playing for the U.S. and off my disappointment at Derby.

I was immediately overwhelmed by the hype already surrounding the team. During press availability time, players were set up at their own "stations" so that the media could come by to do interviews. Most of the press didn't follow the sport and there was a lot of educating to be done. Very few seemed to be interested in talking about the abilities of the players or the game itself. It was mostly about "personalities." I was particularly taken aback by the change in attitude and atmosphere from the '90 World Cup. I was glad we were getting more press, but it created a circus environment and some guys seemed distracted by it all. Having come from a more controlled environment, I didn't know what to think.

I was experiencing some culture shock, too, and I generally felt out of it on every level. Physically, I was dead and in the ice bath after every training session. My body was telling me to pack it in, and that's not how I wanted to feel because I wanted to be at my peak going into the World Cup, not struggling. I had to learn to pace myself, but I still had to perform in training.

Cindi and I went for a long walk around Dana Point, the resort south of Newport Beach where the U.S. team was staying. I tried to put into words what was wrong with me, but I was having a hard time. We talked about my leaving the Premiership to go to Derby and how that hadn't turned out the way I wanted. We talked about everything that had gone on between Trevor and me and how that had tainted my final days with Sheffield. And we talked about what was happening at the World Cup. Even though I was one of the most experienced members of the team, and wanted to contribute in any way I could, I had been away for some time—certainly during the buildup to the World Cup—and for that reason felt like I was having a hard time fitting in. Cindi helped me talk through everything and, more importantly, put it behind me. I got everything off my chest, got my priorities straight, and finally felt focused and ready.

The team chemistry was relatively good. Six or seven of us were coming back from Europe and, once we arrived, Bora had to fit us into a team that had been living and playing together for most of the year. That's not an easy thing to do. Each of us had to learn quickly what Bora was trying to do, and understand and accept our roles.

Looking back, you could say that Bora was the right man for the job at the time. He was supposed to get us to the second round—an ambitious goal—and he did. That was quite an accomplishment and Bora deserves credit for it.

Bora was originally from Yugoslavia, had been everywhere, spoke several languages, and most importantly, had been exposed to international soccer as both a player and a manager. That experience gave him unquestionable credibility with the players, although we weren't always sure what to make of him. Bora was very disciplined and, although he liked to have fun, it was hard to know when he was kidding around or being serious. He kept everyone guessing.

On the field, Bora had strong feelings about how we should play: keep it simple, build out of the back, and draw the opposition out. Let them chase after us, keep the score down, and take advantage of opportunities when they arose. One thing Bora did very well was give confidence to the younger players—especially Cobi and Alexi—who had been with him for the full year.

Another smart move on Bora's part was to make the World Cup a celebration for the team. Our families were allowed to see us at the resort and were included in many of the activities. Rather than distract us, having our families there helped us relax and made us feel part of what was going on. We could feel the excitement, and that helped us get ready to play.

Some players and commentators thought that the way Bora had us play was too conservative and boring. I certainly

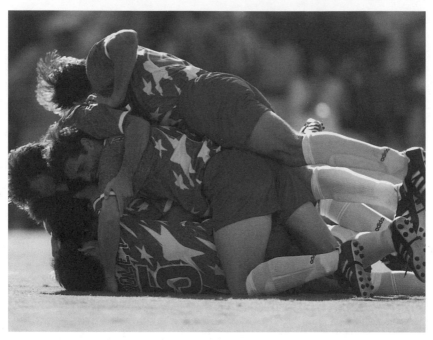

*Celebrating Ernie Stewart's goal in 2–1 win over Colombia
in the '94 World Cup.*

would have preferred more balance in our attack, probably because I was coming from England where the style of play was so direct. Some of the press didn't like Bora because he was sometimes evasive and distant, so they probably would have criticized him no matter what. Although the players were much more confident and experienced in 1994 than in 1990, and could have played the ball more forward (as we started to do in 1995), it's important to remember that in 1994 the U.S. wasn't respected by many countries and we still had to play smart, cautious football to be successful. But no matter what anyone had to say about Bora's coaching or tactics, no one can argue with his results, the first of which came in our opening game against Switzerland.

A chartered jet took us from L.A. to Detroit for the opening game. The jet had open flooring, couches, a buffet, and our own flight attendants. That may be part of an average day in the life of the Chicago Bulls, but the U.S. team was used to flying strictly coach. It was a nice touch by the Federation, and the special treatment made us feel important and boosted our confidence. I captured the scene on videotape and had a lot of fun interviewing the players. The National Team card school was going strong, and Brad Friedel and some of the boys had a big game going on the flight. It was very different from 1990, and we took it all in. When we arrived at the airport, it was packed with U.S. fans—another new experience.

I was rooming with Tony Meola and it seemed like he was on the phone 20 hours a day. His agent was calling all the time to talk about everything from kicking field goals for the Jets to reading movie scripts. He was also one of the players who had been with Bora all year, and he'd taken over as captain when Peter Vermes was cut, so he was constantly busy. Tony and I were good roommates, and I was able to keep his new-found fame in perspective with a few well-timed wisecracks. But the thing I remember most clearly about the night before the Switzerland game is O.J. on the run in his white Bronco. I was glued to the TV until midnight, before I started to think that I should probably get some sleep. Tony watched the coverage until 1:00 in the morning, like most of the country. He finally shut it off and then his wife, Colleen, called at 2:00 A.M. The whole night was surreal and not the way I usually prepare for a match.

Going into the Switzerland match, emotions were running high, and we didn't know what to expect from the American crowd. It was also strange to have the first game of the World Cup played indoors in the Silverdome. A high-tech, grass tray system had been installed, pieced together over the astroturf, and it held up pretty well. Once the game got started, we were breathing pretty hard and feeling the heaviness of the indoor air—not enough circulation. But playing a World Cup match at home made up for it. I couldn't believe how much the U.S. fans were into the game.

Chances in the Switzerland match still stick out in my mind. Both Thomas Dooley and Ernie Stewart had opportunities. The team was playing well and, more importantly, we

1994 World Cup.

were playing with confidence. Georges Bregy scored for Switzerland in the 40th minute on a 19-yard free kick that was awarded to the Swiss after Thomas Dooley took down Alain Sutter just outside the box. But five minutes later, I got the ball played to me and I took off on a run. As I went past one player, another ran at me from the side. When I was about 25 yards out, and just as the other player was about to get to the ball, I used my body enough for him to foul me. Now it was our turn to take a free kick.

Tab and I were around the ball, and Eric Wynalda stepped up and said, "I've got to hit this one, I feel it. Just let me hit this one." We didn't argue given the look on his face. The crowd quieted down a bit, Waldo took a few steps and struck the ball. At first it seemed like it was going to sail over the goal, but then it dipped into the top corner. The keeper dove right and it looked like he was there to get it, but it was just out of his reach. That goal must have come from the heavens. It was out of this world; one of the best free kicks I've ever seen. Eric took off celebrating and I just stood there, shocked. It took me a second to grasp what had happened, and then I started to chase after him along with the rest of the team. We couldn't believe it. The crowd erupted and the cheers echoed inside the Silverdome. *"USA! USA! USA!"* It was so satisfying to receive that kind of support at home in the States.

Emotionally, the whole team was flying after we tied Switzerland 1–1. There was a reception after the game and Chris Waddle was there doing some work for the BBC. Cindi's and my family were there too. After playing for so long in England, away from so many family members and friends, it was great to be able to share the game with people who were important to me and to play in front of a true home crowd again.

On the charter back to California, some guys were playing cards, Tab was calculating results and points, and others decided to take a nap—not a wise move around this group of players—and most woke up with food and other objects on their heads. After training a couple of days at Mission Viejo, we went to Pasadena to prepare for our second game against Colombia at the Rose Bowl. Once the games started, we were kept a little more isolated, but at least when we were in Dana Point, we could go for walks, shop, and keep things fairly normal. In Pasadena we were restricted to the hotel and about all we could do was get together in one of the rooms and watch the other games. It's hard to keep yourself entertained all day in a hotel.

As a team, we were lucky to get along so well. It was like Sheffield, in a way, except that we didn't get to play with each other on a regular basis. Playing with the National Team is completely different from being with your club team, or even other professional sports, where you're on the road for a few days here and there. Between tournaments, training, and trips to other countries, once the National Team players finally get together, we're often around each other for weeks at a time. And that's not easy. But we got on well, had the same sense of humor, and enjoyed a lot of laughs. More importantly, we respected each other and were totally committed to the team and to being successful. No matter what it took.

Everybody knew how important the World Cup was to helping the American public become familiar with soccer and the guys who were playing it. But the soccer market in America was tricky—still is—and big sponsors were not in a hurry to lay down dollars for relatively unknown players. Trying to make people understand the difference between the National Team and the Olympic team was hard enough, let alone getting investors to put their money behind a sport that received minimal coverage in the papers and was almost never seen on TV.

It was a big help to the U.S. team to be based in Southern California because the television people were around us a lot. "The Tonight Show" was hanging around and ESPN and MTV were doing interviews. It was the kind of coverage that we'd never had, a huge increase in exposure. Of course, a lot of the media had no idea who we were or what it was they were covering, which was frustrating, but at least they were physically there. It was a nice change from the small handful of journalists who were usually around.

While the World Cup organizers did an awesome job from a marketing point of view, a lot of players felt misled about what would be in it for them individually. Everyone had dreams of major sponsorships. Along with the sudden attention, there were a lot of changes in terms of how the players thought about themselves and how much market value they had. Everybody was fighting for their little piece of the pie. It was the first big marketing test for players. But for players like Paul Caligiuri, Marcelo Balboa, Tab, Eric, and me—those of us who had been around for the long haul—the words "soccer" and "market value" had never been used in the same sentence.

Suddenly everybody was getting agents, as if there was this one great opportunity that might not ever come around again and no one wanted to miss out. Who's going to market me? Who should I sign with? Which agent should I get? I had never had anybody represent me in the States, so I was completely out of the American representation loop. And most of the European guys weren't able to be marketed in the States before the World Cup simply because we had been overseas. All the players who were based in the U.S., however, were making local appearances and getting the most out of soccer's moment in the limelight.

Still, some of the major advertising spots didn't even use actual U.S. players, which was a wasted opportunity for both the team and the sport. But personalities were beginning to develop and we were getting some mainstream coverage. Among other things, I was featured in *Sports Illustrated* and named as one of *People* magazine's 50 Most Beautiful People of 1994. I got a good laugh out of that. Alexi was getting a lot of attention for his red hair and goatee. Lexi's very down-to-earth—he'd be the first to tell you that the attention took him by surprise—and he took all the sudden attention and pressure in stride. All the players got together in the hotel to watch him as a guest on "The Tonight Show" and "David Letterman." He did well—even trimmed his beard on t.v.—and that was a big step for U.S. soccer. We didn't care what show it was or who was on it, as long as the sport and the players were getting exposure.

After tying Switzerland, the media hype surrounding the team as we headed into the Colombia game was even more intense. Colombia was a big favorite to win, and even Pele had been quoted in the paper saying that Colombia could win the whole tournament. While the rest of the world may not have agreed, we believed that we had it in us to beat them. Even so, we were surprised—and so was the rest of the world—when we actually did.

Over 100,000 people poured into the Rose Bowl—an atmosphere that's impossible to describe—and once the match started, we were pumped up to play. As the game went on and we matched them all over the pitch, we became more confident and started to have fun. We started to take the game to them a bit, instead of sitting back and playing for the tie. Right before we scored our first goal in the 35th minute, Paul Caligiuri, who was playing behind me, fed me the ball out wide. When I was about 25 yards out, I cut inside on my right, came back on to my left side again, and thought, "What the hell—I'll just whack it across the goal and see what happens."

All the members of the media asked me afterward, "Was that a shot?" I told them that it wasn't and that I hit it, basically, because it was there. In England I was taught to put the ball into the box because that's the danger area. I knew players would be making runs toward the goal, so I just whacked it in there hard. I saw Andres Escobar stretch back to get it, and then I saw Ernie Stewart at the back post. I think Ernie would have gotten to the ball if Escobar hadn't, but it just slid off of Escobar and went into the net: an own goal. As soon as I saw that, I turned around and I didn't know where to start celebrating first so I ran toward the U.S. bench. Everybody came out and piled on top of me, even though I hadn't scored.

In the second half, we were playing well and started to control the game more. Tab chipped a beautiful ball through to Ernie which he ran onto and smoothly slipped past the keeper, inside the near post. It turned out to be the winning goal. Colombia did manage to score on us toward the end of the game, but the moment was ours. It was more than I ever could have imagined, winning 2–1 at home against Colombia in the Rose Bowl. There we were, the underdogs at home, and we not only pulled off an incredible upset, but the U.S. won its first World Cup match in over 40 years in front of 100,000 people. After the final whistle blew, I walked around the field with the rest of the team, the American flag draped over us, trying to soak up every moment. Bringing home a win for your country when competing at the highest level— especially when no one anywhere thinks you stand a chance—is a rush that's hard to describe.

Sadly, Escobar paid for that own goal with his life when he returned home to Colombia. He was shot for what someone believed was an unforgivable mistake. The game lost a great player because a very disturbed individual took his passion for his country too far. Escobar's death obviously redirected my and the other players' thoughts and feelings about our win. It's something that I have never forgotten, especially since I played a role in the events that occurred on the field.

Papers everywhere gave the U.S. win huge play, and the soccer world was stunned. For us, it was one of the biggest wins in our history, and it gave the team a big publicity boost. Ernie Stewart became the first—and only—soccer player ever to grace the cover of *Sports Illustrated*.

We had one more game to play, against Romania, and if the other results in the group went our way, we had a chance of getting to the second round. And after beating Colombia, we were on an even bigger high than after the Switzerland game. We thought we could beat Romania, and we probably should have. We had some good chances. I hit the post, as did Eric and Alexi, and Marcelo just missed on a number of headers. Instead, we lost 1–0. Even though it was a frustrating loss, we were headed to the second round of the World Cup. Just four years earlier we had made news with our respectable 1–0 loss to Italy. Now, we had tied Switzerland, beaten Colombia, and were going to the second round of the World Cup along with only 15 other teams. It was another giant leap forward for U.S. soccer. However, it was a bittersweet—and short—celebration for me.

In the Romania game, I got my second yellow card of the tournament, while standing in the wall as Romania took a free kick. Hagi complained that we had moved up a few steps, and I was the unlucky one who got booked because I was standing closest to the ref. Advancing to the second round was an amazing accomplishment for us, and I wanted to be there. I was worried that two yellow cards were going to get me suspended from the next match, but right after the game the ref walked over to let me know that I had nothing to worry about. The cards weren't going to carry over into the second round and I would be clear to play against Brazil, our second round opponent.

I walked off the field, showered, and walked out of the locker room where the entire press corps was waiting to pounce on me. I wasn't quite sure why. Finally, a reporter

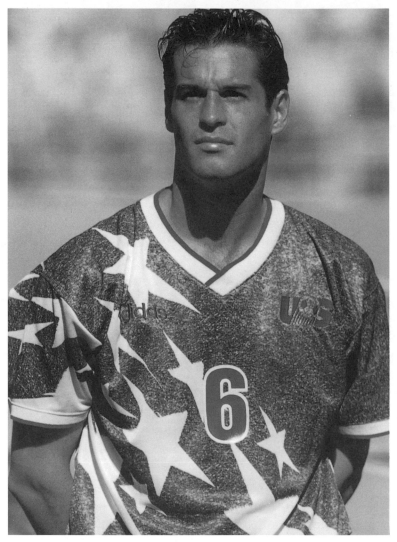

Before the Colombia match.

asked me, "John, how does it feel to be suspended from the Brazil game?"

I didn't know what to say and thought he must have been mistaken. But if that was true, all the other reporters were under the same impression as he was. I had no idea what was going on. Bora, Sunil Gulati, everyone was trying to chase down FIFA officials for an explanation, but they couldn't get hold of anyone in a position of authority. The media was still on top of me, asking for a reaction, and I didn't know what I was supposed to be reacting to. After what the ref had told me, I was stunned that suspension was even a possibility. Then, in the middle of all the chaos, I heard a voice come over the intercom in the Rose Bowl announcing that I had been suspended from the next game.

I was distraught, totally torn apart. My first and possibly only chance to play in the second round of the World Cup, a match against Brazil on the fourth of July in front of a home crowd in Palo Alto, and I wasn't going to be able to do it. It killed me, especially because the yellow cards weren't justified.

So instead of playing against Brazil, I was given a small, handheld camera by ESPN to capture some behind-the-scenes moments of the Brazil game, which was good because it gave me something to do besides fume over being suspended. I shot some video in the locker room and talked to players about how it felt to be playing against Brazil. Just talking to my teammates about the game was difficult enough, but that was nothing compared to having to watch the match from the bench. I knew the important thing was for me to stay positive and be supportive because that was what the boys needed. We had our work cut out for us against the Brazilians, and the game was very physical. By design, it was also a very defensive game for us, and a lot of responsibility was falling on the back line. But they held their own, clearing shots off the line and making the right tackles. And we had one or two good chances offensively, too.

At the end of the first half, Tab was on the opposite side of the field with Leonardo and they were battling for the ball. They were far away, but I could see Leonardo crack Tab in the skull with his elbow. Tab went down hard. And then I saw him have what looked like a convulsion and I jumped up—the whole bench did. We could see then that he was badly injured. All the guys on the field were yelling and motioning to the trainers, Rudy Rudowski and Hughie O'Malley,

133

to get out there. This was no dive, and the trainers sprinted across the field. All I could see from the bench was Tab lying on the ground, twitching.

They put him on a stretcher and took him to the locker room, and I followed them in. At first I was relieved that I couldn't see blood anywhere, and I thought maybe things weren't as bad as they appeared. But when I looked down at Tab's face, I knew he was seriously hurt. He was very groggy and couldn't focus his eyes at all. The entire side of his face looked damaged and swollen. I asked him if he was okay and all he could manage to say was that he was struggling. I stayed with him in the locker room and clutched his arm. He was that scared, and I was scared for him, although I didn't want him to know that.

While we were waiting, and after the doctors had finished their initial examination, I could hear them speak in low voices to each other about Tab's condition. I heard one of them say, "He might be bleeding internally. We've got to keep him on his side in case there's any damage to the brain." That scared the hell out of me and I prayed that Tab couldn't hear them. I stayed with Tab for a while and about 20 minutes into the second half he told me that he was all right and I should go back out to be with the team.

Up until that point, we had been doing well. But now we were on our heels and we had to make changes. Our fate was sealed by an agonizing goal by Bebeto. Competing against Brazil, we were all expecting some mind-blowing shot, an unstoppable rocket. Not this time. The goal seemed to come out of nowhere, without much of a build-up. Romario slipped it to Bebeto, who ran in, went wide of Lexi, and slipped the ball past Tony, who was already committed. It was an off-pace goal that looked like it was happening in slow motion. Sometimes when the other team scores, even though you're not thrilled, your reaction is, "*That* was a great goal." It's as if to say there was nothing that could be done about it. It was a quality shot. But when Bebeto's shot went into the net, all of us sitting on the bench dropped our heads. I hated having to sit there, unable to help the team. That was the only goal Brazil managed to score, but it was enough, and we lost 1–0. The World Cup was over for us. By the time we got back to the locker room after the game, Tab had already been taken away for tests. A few of the doctors who had gotten a look at him said that his injury was one of the worst they'd seen in soccer and that he might not play again.

After the game, there was a reception set up for us in a restaurant across from the stadium. We weren't feeling that great because of the result and Tab's injury. But deep down we were proud of ourselves because, although we lost, it was only 1–0 to Brazil, the team that went on to win the World Cup. Cindi and Tab's wife, Amy, had gone to the hospital to be with him. After the game, Leonardo, who had been ejected from the game, went to visit him. He apologized, and brought Tab his game jersey. It didn't change anything, but it was a nice gesture on Leonardo's part.

At the reception, we were all standing around talking about the game, when Robin Williams suddenly walked into the room. He started cracking jokes and soon everyone there was laughing. He also spoke seriously for a few minutes about how much it meant to him, as a fan, to witness what we had accomplished. I was excited because having him there made me feel like soccer was finally working its way into the mainstream. I mean, this was Mrs. Doubtfire, for God's sake, telling us *he* followed *us*!

After the reception, it was back to the hotel to get my things packed. The next day at Dana Point we got some reports about Tab, and learned that he had, in fact, fractured his skull. He'd been released and was coming back to the hotel, but he still felt very uncomfortable.

Bora called a team meeting the day after the game. He came into the rec room that had been set up for us and started talking about how proud he was. We'd done exceptionally well, and as a team we had showed not only our country, but the world, that we could play with the best. And in the process, we'd earned a lot of respect and could leave the tournament with our heads held high. Then he paused, and it was a long pause. Uncomfortable, really. We all looked at him, waiting for him to say something else, and then we noticed he was upset, crying. Then he turned and left the room—just walked out. We couldn't tell if he was joking with us, because you never knew what was going to happen with Bora. We sat there wondering what had happened and whether or not we should leave, too. But he came back in five minutes later saying, "I'm sorry, I'm sorry . . . " He spoke for a few more minutes, some players said a few nice things, and that was it. End of tournament.

Afterward, a few of us hung out for a couple of days at Dana Point. Tab was still having headaches. Cindi and I went to dinner with him and Amy, and he was having a tough time. Tab had fought back from other injuries, but it was obviously going to take a lot for him to recover from this one, not just physically, but mentally, too.

Tab's a fiery spirit; it's hard to keep him down. That's his character and I respect him for that. He's so important to the National Team and has been for such a long time. We were very lucky that wasn't his last game.

Most of the soccer hype ended as soon as the World Cup was over. For the National Team, the commercial success of the event had to be followed by success on the field. But it didn't look like Bora would be a part of it. Reports in the press indicated there was concern within the Federation that Bora wouldn't be able to be fully involved at all levels of youth soccer development, and that's what they expected. Cindi and I went to Jersey and then to Virginia for a couple of days, and after that it was back over to England to get ready for another season at Derby. The '94 World Cup was almost like my first Cup Final at Wembley: an unforgettable experience that came and went too fast.

When you decide to play for a club, like any other choice you might make in your career, you rarely get everything you want in one place. There's always a compromise. You can be happy off the field, but the football is not so good. Or the football can be very good, but you're not settled off the field. At Sheffield Wednesday I had both. At Derby I had neither, and that wasn't a situation I was happy with.

Coming back from all the excitement surrounding the World Cup, Derby took a while to get used to again. We were still stuck in the First Division and there was a cloud hanging over the club. My teammates gave me a good reception my first day back, and congratulated me on the U.S. performance in the World Cup. But overall, the mood was pretty low and the season turned out to be very up-and-down. Managers and directors changed. Players came and went, sold off just a year after the club had invested close to 12 million pounds on buying them and others. There was constant speculation about who would be the next to go, including where and when I would be leaving. It wasn't a settled year for anybody, and it showed in our performance. The fans were sure to let us know it, too. I never had my car trashed or anything that severe, but there were times—too many times—when I'd go

139

One of the many challenges in Division 1.

out at night and fans would come up to me and tell me I was crap and the team was crap. That got old real fast.

I felt stuck. I'd just played in the World Cup and suddenly I was back in the blue-collar First Division, digging it out, trying to get results every week. I thought about moving to another club where I might have a better chance of playing in the Premier League again. Compared to Sheffield and the World Cup, Derby was definitely a grounding experience.

The club went to Denmark for a week of preseason training, and while I was there I found out that "the new American league" wasn't going to start up as planned in 1995. It seemed everyone who was directly involved in the venture had known that for a while—even before the World Cup—but until then I had only heard rumors that the launch would be delayed a year.

I was surprised and, like most American players, I was disappointed by the delay. Although I wasn't ready to leave England yet—I didn't feel like I had done everything I wanted to do—a top-level professional league in America was crucial. I was shocked that after the World Cup, and all of the hype that it created, the crowds that turned out, and the success of the National Team, that the league's organizers couldn't pull it off in 1995. The platform was there, but would it still be there in 1996? On the upside, the delay took away, for the time being at least, any distraction from my career in England. I wanted to get back into the Premier League—every player did—but it didn't look like Derby could do it.

If 1995 was a disappointing year for me at Derby, it was a very big year for the National Team. After our success at the World Cup, many players took advantage of new opportunities to play overseas, while the team as a whole did its best to maintain the momentum we had created in 1994. Eric went to Germany, Lexi went to Italy, Cobi went to England. It was a challenge for us, the next few times that we got together to play, to produce impressive results. Our first, big post-World Cup tournament was U.S. Cup '95. We won the whole thing, just after Bora resigned and Steve Sampson, an assistant at the time, was named interim coach. The highlight was our 4–0 victory over Mexico in front more than 38,000 at RFK Stadium in D.C. We needed that kind of performance, and it helped get us psyched to go down to Uruguay the next month to compete in Copa America, the oldest soccer tournament in the world and the unofficial South American championship. It was great to be invited, but we knew the competition— Brazil, Argentina, and Colombia—was going to be tough.

There were a lot of things that we went down to Uruguay to prove. On a personal level, individual players wanted to solidify their positions on the team. Those who were on and off the squad wanted to secure a regular spot. As a team, we were still dealing with the departure of Bora, and that had a big impact on how we played in Copa America. We also knew that every game we played was a chance to prove to the rest of the world that the U.S. was competitive internationally and that our performance in the World Cup wasn't a fluke.

But before we could prove ourselves on the field, we had to sort out some serious financial and contractual problems that we were having with the Federation. Before we left, we were under the impression that our compensation had been agreed to. But right before we boarded the plane to Paysandu, the Federation faxed a schedule to Marcelo Balboa, our captain at the time, telling us what our pay would be for the tournament. National Team players are generally paid on a per-game basis, with higher appearance fees going to starters and less for substitutes. Usually, there are also team bonuses if we advance far enough in a tournament. The appearance fees and team bonuses the Federation was offering were not what we thought had been agreed to. Celo worked his way down the aisle of the plane, giving everyone the bad news. By the time we landed, everybody was fuming, not just because the amounts were not what we expected, but because of the way the Federation was treating us, and had been treating us for some time.

After we got settled in our rooms, the players had a meeting to discuss how we were going to handle the situation. We had a choice: fight now, or play now and fight later. For various reasons, we decided to draw the line then, even though we knew the tournament was important to us and we weren't certain that rocking the boat was the best thing for us or the Federation.

But we had advanced to the second round of the World Cup and had not been paid very well, considering that the Federation made tens of millions of dollars from the event. Also, for a lot of guys at the time, the money that they made from the National Team was a significant percentage of their income, and a few thousand dollars made a difference to them. For me and the other players who had been on the team for a while, the dispute was about respect—about not being taken for granted or dictated to like children—and also about building a better working relationship between the Federation and future players. These issues had been brewing for a while, and the Federation's lowballing of our Copa compensation was the final straw.

Making matters worse, we were down in Uruguay with an interim coach who was not in a position to assert himself or influence the negotiations. Steve Sampson had been Bora's assistant during the 1994 World Cup, and we were surprised that he was in the running for the permanent job, because he had no real experience. But Steve was in the right place at the right time—not to mention that he spoke fluent Spanish—and he was the man who would be coaching us through Copa America.

Steve quickly earned the players' support. Back then, he seemed to respect our abilities and experience, and we responded really well to that. Steve was a big switch from Bora, and a lot of the players who had been with Bora for such a long period of time were ready for a change. Steve didn't do anything revolutionary, he simply reacted to what Bora had done before him. Steve knew that Bora had played a very defensive system, and he told us that we were free to open things up a bit more when we played. But he didn't pretend to be something he was not. He knew most of us had more experience than he did, and his attitude was, "You guys know what to do. I'm not going to tell you how to play. Use your own instincts, because that's what got you here in the first place." Steve also helped himself in Uruguay when he praised the players for sticking together and fighting the Federation for what we thought was right.

After our initial meeting, we faxed the Federation with our concerns. For the next few days, faxes flew back and forth and there were a lot of phone calls too, mostly through Tom King, who had just joined the team as General Manager and who was down there with us. Tom acted as a go-between and I'm sure he wondered what he'd gotten himself into. The initial offers that the Federation made were not what we expected. The longer the negotiating went on, the more frustrated we got, and the more certain we were that we weren't going to back down until we received a reasonable offer.

It was a shame that our contract negotiations had to take place during Copa, because staying in Paysandu was an unforgettable experience. We stayed in a poverty-stricken area—families living in alleys, young girls sitting on the sidewalk tending to their babies—and even though most of the senior players were used to spending time in underdeveloped countries, it was still a shock when we first arrived. But the people were incredible, and we developed a real affection for the city. We stayed in a very old hotel, right in the middle of town, with big glass windows that faced out onto the street. People stood on the street for hours watching us hang out in the lobby or the lounge—which is where we spent most of our time because our rooms were really small—playing cards, watching TV, and drinking cappuccinos. By around three in the afternoon, after drinking about eight or nine cappuccinos each, we were bouncing off the walls. We'd sit in the lobby, order a drink, and then give the waiter the room number of an unsuspecting teammate. We'd nail somebody different every day. One morning, Mike Burns came down to breakfast and said, "Okay, gentlemen, I just bought 42 cappuccinos. Who did it?"

When we did venture outside the hotel, to look around or go shopping, we were swarmed. I had rarely experienced anything like that with the National Team. As soon as one player would walk outside the hotel, all you could hear was, "Please, please, please . . . Do you have a pin? Do you have a hat? Do you have a badge?" We took turns being the first one to step out the front doors of the hotel. Every day we'd see the same kids asking for autographs—some of them must have gotten 15 autographs from each of us. After a week, it seemed like every little kid walking down the street was decked out in U.S.A. gear.

Our first game of the tournament was against Chile on a Saturday and, as of Thursday morning, we hadn't gotten anywhere with the Federation. Their latest offer was still unacceptable, so we counteroffered again. We were supposed to get a response back that night, but we heard nothing. So Friday morning, the day before our first game, we didn't show up to training. The coaching staff was there, but the players weren't. We wanted to send a message to the Federation that, if they weren't going to negotiate with us, we weren't going to play for them. And if we didn't play for the Federation, it was going to lose a lot of money. That was the first time the Federation understood how serious and committed we were.

At about 3:00 Friday afternoon, a fax finally came through, but it was far from what we were looking for. We knew the best way to prove our point was to stand our ground, and the faxing continued on and on for hours. We had a team meeting scheduled for 6:30 that night and a team dinner at 7:00. The time for the meeting came and went and we were still in the hotel's business center responding to faxes and phone calls.

The team went to a local restaurant for dinner, and when we got back to the hotel Tab and I got a call from Sunil. Tab answered the phone, talked to him for a while, and then got angry and handed the phone to me. Both sides were frustrated and the hours were slipping by. After every phone call or fax, there was a team meeting in someone's room. We'd walk down the hall knocking on doors, and cram the entire team into one tiny room. As it got later and later Friday night, players were starting to get squirmy, wondering, "Are we really not stepping onto the field tomorrow?" But we had come too far to back down. We were unified and determined to prove our point and win this fight.

Tab, Brad Friedel, Celo, Lexi, and I were all in a room with Tom King, who was on the phone trying to track down Hank Steinbrecher and Alan Rothenberg. Tom was still dealing with a lot of the phone calls and our discussions with him got more heated the longer it dragged on. Even though we were acting as a team, none of us wanted to be the one to actually get on the phone, so once we reached Hank, we decided to take turns speaking with him. It was stupid and we didn't get very far. Tom was getting angry and started to play to our sense of national pride. He said that we were treating the National Team like any other club team, and asked us, "How can you disrespect your National Team, and your country?"

Most of the players thought Tom's appeal was patronizing. Of course we knew wearing the National Team uniform was a special privilege. Ask any member of any national team anywhere in the world. Ask an Olympic athlete. They will all tell you that no level of competition compares to the feeling that comes from representing your country. It would be an honor to walk on the field in Paysandu—or anywhere else—and we knew that better and had more experience with it than anyone at the Federation. But if representing your country is such an honor, then we should be treated with a certain amount of respect for doing it. We wanted to be treated like an important part of the sport, both then and in the future. We'd earned that.

The night wore on and the Federation threatened to ship us home and send down the Olympic team in our place. We knew that would ruin the U.S. chances of making an impression in the tournament, and we were insulted, because we knew it would cost them more to send the Olympic team down than it would to give us the bonuses we were asking for. After that threat, we really started worrying about the possible repercussions the dispute could have on our careers. We knew that, if they wanted to, the Federation could try to

146

do just about anything, including kicking one or more of us off the team for good. I knew I should try and control my temper, but I got so frustrated at one point that I just flat out told Tom, "You guys can't do things like that."

"How do you know we can't?"

"I know."

"What do you mean you know?"

"I just know."

And with that, Tab started laughing and fell off the end of the bed and onto the floor. And I'm saying to him, "Tab, come on—we're trying to be serious here." And he was hiding under the bed, still in hysterics. It was one of those moments when the tension is so unbelievably high that only laughter can break it, even if it seems inappropriate at the time. Of all the time we spent arguing and negotiating, faxing, and passing the phone back and forth, I remember that scene the best and it still makes me laugh.

We stuck it out and stood our ground, and the offer that finally satisfied the team arrived at 12:30 A.M. We told the rest of the guys that we were on for our match the next day against Chile, and we slipped a note under Steve's door, letting him know that we were prepared to play. Then we tried to get some sleep.

We felt like we had earned some respect, but we had also taken a risk and boxed ourselves into a corner. We knew that we had to prove to the Federation and ourselves that we were worth what we had been battling for. But that was when this group of guys was at its best, when we had our backs up against the wall.

Riding in the bus on the way to the stadium for the first match, we had a sixth sense that Copa would be one of the best tournaments of our career. We were proud that we had stuck together and fought for something we believed in. It was a small victory, but an important one, and we were psyched. Now we could get on with what we did best—play soccer. Once we arrived at the stadium and started to warm up in the tunnel, we were like little kids at camp, yelling and grunting. We were soaked with sweat before we even stepped out onto the field. We couldn't wait.

We surprised Chile—and the rest of the world—by winning 2–1. We'd never beaten Chile on our own turf, never mind in South America. After winning that game, the crowd clapped us off the field. We followed up the Chile performance by crushing Argentina, 3–0, an historic victory. We won our group and advanced to the semifinals where we had to face Brazil. We hadn't played them since the loss in the World Cup. We lost 1–0—again—but we played well. After that loss, some members of the media stated that Brazil wasn't really playing full throttle, but a 1–0 loss to the World Cup champion was very respectable. By the time we faced Colombia for 3rd place, we were a depleted team and lost 4–1, which was disappointing after our win over them in the World Cup. We played extremely well throughout the tournament and when it was over, I was voted co-MVP alongside Uruguay's Enzo Francescoli, one of the greatest honors I've ever received.

We got our bonus money, but more importantly we put the Federation on notice that the players wouldn't be pushed around anymore. The team learned a lot and changed a lot, both from the on-field results and the camaraderie that developed off the field because of the confrontation. Copa was when the players came together and created a bond that would carry over into 1996 and the beginning of qualifying for World Cup '98.

Our results at Copa also helped Steve Sampson get the head coaching job on a permanent basis. None of us—especially me—realized what effect that decision would later have on the team.

Cobi celebrating with me after beating Argentina in the Copa America.

The best thing about Derby was that my son, Ian, was born there. Otherwise, I'd had enough disappointment and frustration. More and more, I was ready to move on, preferably to a Premier League club, or possibly to the new U.S. professional league if that was a realistic option.

MLS was supposed to start up in the spring of 1996 and, slowly, players were beginning to sign up. The very first player to sign was Tab, and when I first heard about it I was shocked. I knew he was thinking of signing and then I saw the headlines. I guess the reason the news surprised me so much was that I knew he was having a really great year with his club, Nuevo Leon, in Mexico. Even though I wanted the league to be a success—we all did—it still sounded like a big risk to me, to leave a successful and solid situation for a venture as uncertain as a new league. So I called Tab and told him that I thought he had a lot of guts to sign. But everybody who signed with MLS took that risk, although not everybody had the options Tab and I and a few others did. I began the conversation with Tab thinking that he might be making a mistake, but by the time I hung up, I'd realized how much I wanted to come back, too, and help soccer grow in this country. It had been a dream of mine, since I was a ball boy for the

Cosmos in the NASL days, to play in a professional league here.

A lot of the players that came back didn't have to be bought, because they were on loan or out of contract with their clubs. But it looked like the league was going to have to buy me, and it looked like the price was going to be pretty hefty by MLS standards, possibly near $1 million. But there was really no way around it if they wanted me. I didn't think it would happen in the league's first year because, at the time, almost no one involved with the league at the highest level was willing to buy back players. They weren't operating with a lot of cash.

In 1995, after all the negotiating, my price came down to about 550,000 pounds. And that was a lot of money—about 900 grand—for MLS to spend at the time. That the league would put out that kind of money for me made me feel wanted and also more secure about the league's finances.

The delay between my signing and the start of the first MLS season gave me a chance to get back into the Premier League. My agent, Mel Stein, set up a deal in 1995 to have MLS buy my rights from Derby and then turn around and loan me out to a mid-level Premiership club, West Ham United, for the 1995–96 season. The way it worked, I would come back for the inaugural MLS season as soon as West Ham no longer feared relegation to the First Division. It was a breath of fresh air to be competing again at the highest level and playing at places like Highbury, Old Trafford, and all the other Premiership grounds that I loved. And, even though Cindi and I had just bought a house, had Ian, and were finally settling in Derby, we were excited to move down to London. We decided to keep the house in Derby, and we found a town house in an area of East London called Butler's Wharf, right on the Thames. Playing in London was incredible, partly because the city itself had so much going on, and also because the competition among the London football clubs and their rivalry with the clubs up north gave me another perspective on English soccer.

Oddly enough, my playing debut after signing with West

Ham was away against Sheffield Wednesday. I didn't start the match, but did get to play. Even before the game started, though, it was a humbling experience for me. As soon as I went out on the field to warm up, I got a standing ovation. I was totally stunned by the reception, especially after being away from Sheffield for two years. Even though I still received fan mail from Sheffield Wednesday supporters, I wondered if the fans would give me a hard time now that I was playing against them. But I think they knew I never wanted to leave Sheffield, and they showed me how much they respected what I had done for the club.

When I finished warming up, I walked over to the sidelines and sat down on the bench with the rest of the players. I looked up and they were staring at me. "Geez, Harkesy, you must have been well-liked here." And, even though I'd never thought about it like that, I said, "Well, apparently I was." It was an incredibly satisfying experience. When it was announced during the game that I would be coming on, the crowd cheered for me again. I was on an emotional high, playing at Sheffield Wednesday and being back up in the Premiership, after such a frustrating experience at Derby.

In a way it was the perfect way to reenter the Premiership. But it was hard, too, because it made me wish that I was back in Sheffield and playing for Wednesday again. But I knew it would never have been the same. Even if I were asked today to go back, I would have to think hard. After everything we achieved there and the chemistry we had, my expectations would be pretty high. Chris Waddle used to say that a footballer might play 10 years, but maybe only five of them would be good. I was so fortunate to have such a fantastic experience on and off the field so early in my career. I played a pretty good game that night, nothing spectacular, but I guess I was inspired to be there and to make my debut for a new club. Afterward, as I was walking off the field, the crowd clapped for me again, and sang—"Ooh, aah, Johnny Harkes, say ooh, aah, Johnny Harkes."—the same chant I used to get when I was playing for Wednesday.

I wondered how many times something like that would

happen to me in my life and decided this was probably it. Sheffield was cheering because they remembered me, West Ham because it was my debut. I also knew the chance was good that I might never play again at Sheffield, especially under those kind of circumstances, so I clapped each of the sections—north, east, south, and west—in the stadium. And then I walked off the center of the field. The entire stadium was clapping for me, and it wasn't because I'd made some brilliant tackle or scored a goal. It was acceptance and it was recognition.

After I showered and changed, I signed autographs long after the game. People were yelling, "John, come back to us! We miss you!" The whole evening was a turning point for me. It made me realize that I had a good career in England, and that realization made me feel more settled about coming back to the States. That night when I got home, I thought, "I can stop now. I'm ready to go home."

The manager at West Ham at the time was Harry Redknapp. Harry was a good coach and I got along with him well. I didn't have time to get really close to a lot of people, but I liked the group of players that were there. Cindi and I hung out often with Iain Dowie and his wife, among others. Iain was the first player in England to get his university degree, something that was unheard of over there. It was then that I started thinking about finishing my degree once I got back to the States. I admired him for making the time to do that, which isn't easy when you have a family and are on the road all the time.

West Ham had a ton of midfielders, so I usually had to play in back. Although I preferred playing in midfield—and have always said so when asked—it has always been more important to me to be on the field and playing where my team needs me most. In West Ham's case, that meant right back.

Combine the number of midfielders with the fact that I was constantly going back and forth between England and the States to play for the National Team, and you have a recipe for life on the bench. Of course, my expected return to

156

the States in March or April for MLS didn't help my playing situation either. Redknapp wasn't about to work me into the team if I was going to be leaving. He needed to have a set team that he could develop and build on, so it was hard for me to get playing time. He'd already made up his mind about me, no matter how I played, and he wasn't concerned about what he could do with me for the 10 or 13 games that he had me. I talked to him about it—I had to—and he was pretty straight with me. He basically said, "Harkesy, what do you want me to do? Put you on the team; you're in for two games and then what? You're going to go back to the States again for this or that tournament and then you're leaving for good, anyway." Not what I wanted hear, but at least he was honest. He was also right.

It was probably something I should have expected going in, but I had to have something while I waited for MLS to start. In January 1996, I finally found myself on a four-game playing streak with West Ham, but was called back to the States to play for the National Team in a tournament in California. During the tournament, I tore my calf muscle. So not only had I left to go back and play for the U.S. again, but I came back injured and was then out of commission for 2½ weeks. Not the ideal situation.

Even though I knew Redknapp didn't want me to, I kept playing for the National Team whenever I could, because I loved to come back to the States and play for my country. That has always been important to me. And Steve Sampson made it clear that he needed me as we geared up for World Cup qualification. He had even flown over to England to tell me in person that he wanted me to be captain. We were at dinner in London with Kasey Keller, Juergen Sommer—both playing in England at the time—and our wives, and after Steve made the announcement, Juergen offered up a very flattering and complimentary toast, which meant a lot to me. At that moment, we were all ready to get on with qualifying and confident that, as a group, we would get it done.

It's hard on a player to be torn between club and country. Players in other professional sports generally don't have to

deal with that kind of conflict, and people are usually surprised when they stop to think about it. The public tends to
think that playing for your national team is so prestigious
that it should be given precedence. But try explaining that to
a club coach in the middle of a season who's trying to avoid
relegation, competing in a Cup tournament, or worried about
losing his job.

The Federation Internationale de Football Association
(FIFA) has rules that prevent a club—as long as there has
been enough notice—from refusing to release a player to ap-
pear in a sanctioned national team game. In friendlies, however, the clubs have more discretion and the player often
ends up caught in the middle. The player is on the club pay-
roll and for that reason the manager feels like the club gets
priority. But if the player's federation tells him the match is
important, the player is going to want to play and will have
to persuade the club to release him. I regularly got the "we're
the ones who pay your wages" speech, which is true and a
good point. But who in their right mind is going to give up a
chance to play for their country?

So I was playing, I wasn't playing. I was in, I was out. It
was hard to give wholeheartedly to West Ham because my
mind was already on moving back to the States. I had never
really felt settled in my play after the '94 World Cup. Everything felt so temporary and uncertain, and it showed in my
performances. I knew I wanted out of Derby, but then when I
got to West Ham I knew I would be leaving. But life off the
field was terrific. We got the most out of everything London
had to offer. We had a constant stream of visitors from
Sheffield and Derby—we loved playing the hosts. We also got
to spend a lot of time with our close friends Pat and Cheryl
Nelson, and the Waddles would come down to join us whenever they could. Ian was also growing fast, and it was fasci-
nating to watch him change from an infant into a toddler.

After I'd finally decided to come back to the States, there
was still speculation whether or not the league was going to
happen in the spring. I had signed on for MLS, so I sure
hoped it would happen. But players were calling and telling

me that there still weren't enough investors or sponsors. I kept thinking about the NASL folding my sophomore year of high school. I thought I would come out of high school, play for the Cosmos, and my life would be set. Then it was gone and I was devastated. For years, a soccer league wasn't even discussed. When MLS came along, I wanted it to work, I dreamed it would work, but there were still doubts and it was making me nervous. It was a waiting game. Waiting for investors, waiting for sponsors, waiting for more guys to sign up. But I'd been waiting for close to 10 years. As players, we were so hopeful, and we had pinned our dreams to the success and future of the league. I didn't want the rug pulled out from under me.

Cindi and I packed up the house in London at the end of March and I had about eight days off before we needed to be back in the States. I was exhausted and I knew that the first MLS season was going to be a long one, on and off the field. Cindi, Ian, and I went to Scotland, where we visited with my relatives before heading back. The opening match was only a week and a half away.

I arrived in D.C. and began training with D.C. United for MLS's inaugural game in San Jose against the Clash on April 6. I was with a new club in a new league preparing for our opening game, and I was back with Bruce Arena. I knew that was going to take a little getting used to. I was used to playing for clubs that had been around for a hundred years and in MLS there was no history, no tradition, no particular way of doing things.

It was also hard to pick myself up mentally and go to work again every day after finishing a season in England. I had been playing soccer nonstop and had picked up some niggling injuries. I hadn't had much of a break during the summer because of my National Team commitments—maybe a week here, 10 days there. In fact, I hadn't had a real vacation since my honeymoon four years earlier. Between playing for my clubs in England, U.S. Cups in the States during the summer, and international friendlies, there hadn't been a lot of free time. And because I had played a full season overseas with Derby and West Ham, I thought I would be match fit when I got back. But I only had four or five days to train with D.C. and when the opening day rolled around, I hadn't yet adjusted to what for me was a dramatic change in my life. In hindsight, I should have come back to the U.S. earlier.

It really hit me while I was standing on the field listening to the National Anthem. All I could think, was, "What am I doing here? How did this happen? Am I really playing back home?" I was thinking about the Premiership and wondering what the level of play would be like. My mind was racing. But I had to be out on that field. Not only for myself, but for the league. After forking over the money to bring me over here, I didn't think MLS wanted me to skip the first game.

We played, we lost. Eric Wynalda—thank God—scored for the Clash late in the second half, because the last thing anyone wanted was a 0–0 tie in the first-ever MLS game, since low-scoring has always been one of the biggest criticisms of soccer in the States. The quality of soccer was mediocre, and the story in *Sports Illustrated* was mostly negative. It was clear that getting decent, mainstream press coverage was going to be an uphill battle.

Life off the field was an adjustment, too. Trying to get settled in the States after being away six years was difficult. The MLS didn't have the kind of resources that the clubs in Europe do to help out. When you move to a new club overseas, the club goes out of their way for you. Three or four people are assigned to you, to make sure you get a car and find a house right away. Luckily, I had bought a town house in the D.C. area two years earlier, but it was empty while we waited for our furniture to be sent from overseas. My whole house in Derby was full, in addition to what we had in the town house in London. Six years of my life was on its way from England and the delivery was delayed for weeks. We were living off paper plates. I'm not complaining—things could've been worse—but the transition was rough. Fortunately, Cindi's parents lived nearby, and they helped out a great deal. But it took time.

After being back for about a month and while I was still

adjusting to the level of play on the field and the frustrations off the field, I wondered if coming back to the States was the right decision. People still ask me if I would have liked to stay in England for another four or five years. I usually answer "yes," but don't know if I mean it. I loved the football side of life in England, but I much prefer living here. My family is here, my friends are here, and I want to bring up my kids here. And we have a great life in America. As much as I loved the football in England, I knew that the life I wanted for my family and me was here. But I was always thinking about the choice that I had made and doing a lot of second-guessing. Maybe I had come back too soon. Either way, I wasn't making it easy on myself.

All smiles with Cindi, Lauren, and Ian.

Signing autographs for Jaime Moreno look-a-likes at D.C. United.

So back here, the challenge was trying to balance every-thing in my new life, and there was a lot to balance. When I was playing in England, how far did I travel? Maybe three hours away by bus; four hours, tops. And I was back the next night. Here we travel for three days—on a plane, flying cross-country, changing time zones—week in and week out. It's much harder. We thought coming home would be great, eas-ier, more comfortable. We'd get settled and I'd play in the new league. But I saw more of Cindi and Ian when I was in England than I did once we came back to the States. My fam-ily is everything to me, and it seemed strange that, once I was finally "back home" in my own country, I would feel further away from them.

On the field, I wasn't under the same kind of pressure as I was in England, but thinking like that made it more difficult for me to do what I needed to do—play my game. Again, it was hard to find a balance. I had to get organized, I had to focus, and more importantly, I had to start to put my life into perspective. On the field and off the field, the way I handled myself had to change. I had to ask myself what I really wanted and what was going to make me happy. For me, the answer was helping make the league a success, qualifying for the World Cup, and building a good life for myself and my family in the States.

I think that a lot of players were in, and are in, similar situations. It was hard that first year because there were a lot of demands put on the National Team players. We had to go beyond the call of duty to sell the game. It wasn't just the level of competition in England that I missed, or the atmosphere at all the games. I'd gotten used to being in a place where soccer was *it*—everywhere, all the time. But when those of us who were playing abroad came back to the States, we were coming back as salesmen and we weren't used to being in a place where the game needed to be sold. A lot of demands were put on the players by the league and by sponsors in terms of marketing and publicity the first season. While I knew that was necessary, I was also thinking, "Hold on a second—we've got to play well first." In the beginning, the product on the field wasn't the best. It can always get better. But everybody knew from the start that if the league was going to succeed, the quality of play had to improve. If we were going to be salesmen, we had to have a good product.

I was lucky that I had close friends around to tell me that I needed to focus solely on my game. Cindi told me, as well. "Would you stop moaning and start playing your game?" I was surprised, at first, and argued that I was playing well. But she told me straight out that I wasn't playing like I did eight months earlier, six months earlier, even four months earlier. "You're not that same player who was sharp and aggressive and going after a game and working hard. You're worrying about too many things." And she was right.

The first month of the season, I was still trying to catch up. I didn't start to get back into any kind of rhythm until probably the second or third week of May. After the first few months, no one would have believed that D.C. United was going to win the championship that year, although I never lost confidence. We started off the season on a losing streak, and didn't really get any results until we started to get used to each other. Things finally began to gel, and June and July flew by. The league was starting to pick up steam in the media, as well. The first MLS All-Star Game in Giants Stadium was a doubleheader in mid-July, also featuring Brazil against the FIFA All Stars, and it set a new attendance record for sporting events in Giants Stadium. The only larger crowd there was for the Pope—it's pretty tough to upstage the Pope. I was selected to play in both games, but because of a hamstring injury, I only played as part of the FIFA All-Stars. It was the biggest event of the year for MLS and an honor for me to have the opportunity to play alongside players like Lothar Matthaeus, Michael Laudrup, and Marcel Desailly. By the time September rolled around, D.C. was headed into the playoffs and I was exhausted from playing two consecutive seasons.

We finished the season in third place in the Eastern Conference, and lost our first playoff game on astroturf in Giants Stadium to the New York/New Jersey MetroStars, a team that we'd developed a great rivalry with in just the first year—exactly what the league needed. It was particularly strange for me playing against Tony, Tab, and Peter Vermes, guys that I've played with from Jersey for years. We got on a roll, beating the MetroStars two straight, and sweeping the Eastern Conference champs, Tampa Bay. The crowds at RFK were knowledgeable and passionate and they got us pumped.

The league's first championship game—MLS Cup '96—will never be forgotten. Near hurricane conditions at Foxboro wasn't what anyone was hoping for. We played the Los Angeles Galaxy in a mud bath, with players sliding all over the place—swimming, more like it—and we were down 2–0 late in the second half. It didn't look like we had much of a chance, but the strange thing was that even as the time ticked away, none of us thought we were going to lose. And we were right. Tony Sanneh and Shawn Medved helped us equalize and then Eddie Pope's "golden goal" in extra time made D.C.

Interviewed by Alexi Lalas during the '96 MLS playoffs.

United the first-ever league champions. As amazing as our comeback was, the fact that almost 35,000 people stood in the downpour—around six inches of rain fell during the weekend—to see it happen was even more mind-blowing. To top things off, we beat the Rochester Rhinos a week later to win the U.S. Open Cup, the oldest club tournament in the United States. We had won the double. It was a good first year for the league as a whole, and for D.C. United in particular. It surpassed a lot of people's expectations and made a lot of critics think twice.

MLS has changed the future of soccer in the States: creating stars, satisfying soccer fans, keeping the sport in the public eye, and giving kids something to aspire to. It will have a favorable impact on the professional, amateur, and youth levels, putting soccer on the map in the States and getting players noticed internationally. Without a doubt, its success is critical to the success of soccer in this country.

165

From the beginning, MLS had an effect on the National Team. Whether the effect was good or bad, at least in the short term, is hard to say. Before the league existed, National Team members would come in for games from all over the place—Germany, England, the Netherlands, and elsewhere. We were all doing well where we were, and our lives were kept pretty separate until we came together to play for the U.S. We weren't competing against one another on a regular basis, on or off the field. But once MLS came into existence, National Team members were competing against each other week in and week out, in our own country. And that competition could be watched and written about every day. Players were also competing with each other for publicity and exposure, something else that hadn't been much of an issue. Everyone wanted to know what everyone else's "deal" was. It was a situation that existed all over the world, but it wasn't one that American players were used to.

Fortunately, the guys on the National Team had really come together during Copa America, and that bond helped us adjust to our new playing relationship. That closeness was also important because after the end of the first MLS season, the first round of qualifying for the 1998 World Cup began. The players' relationship with the Federation was as tense as ever because in 1996 we began renegotiating the National Team contract–per game appearance fees, World Cup bonuses, group licensing rights, sponsorships, promotions, and all sorts of other things. Everyone wanted to get the new contract signed before the first round of qualifying started in November 1996, but things weren't going very well.

Early in 1996, the players had hired lawyers for the first time: Mel Stein, my former agent in the U.K., and Mark Levinstein, a D.C. attorney who'd had a lot of experience with sports law. The Federation wasn't too happy that the players had retained counsel, but we thought it was important, after our experience in Uruguay, to have a buffer between us and the people we were negotiating with. Brad Friedel, Kasey Keller, Alexi Lalas, Mike Burns, and I—as captain—were selected by the team as player reps, so in addition to representing the players' views to Steve, I was also helping represent the players' views to the Federation. Negotiations continued through the summer and into the fall, and during that time the U.S. competed in the U.S. Cup and a friendly or two, one game at a time, under the terms of our old agreement. Although the amount of the players' appearance fees and World Cup bonuses were part of the negotiations, the main issue was that we, as players, wanted to establish more of a "partnership" with the Federation. We specifically wanted to share in the Federation's sponsorship and other revenues in return for becoming more involved in the Federation's marketing activities. Through our new players' association, we'd help get new sponsors, make more appearances, help increase match attendance, and get involved in other promotional efforts. We thought we could help make the sport grow—increase the size of the "soccer pie"—and we wanted to take on more responsibility and expand the relationships that were there. Actually, by the end of June we had made good progress, and the Federation had agreed to share licensing revenues and gate receipts in return for the players getting more involved in marketing the team and promoting individual games. After the Olympics, though, Alan Rothenberg stepped in and took the shares in licensing and gate receipts off the table.

Things came to a head at the end of September when the Federation cut off negotiations and sent new contracts to 82 players—not even acknowledging the existence of our lawyers—and threatened players to sign or risk being left off the roster for both a mid-October friendly against Peru and the first World Cup qualifier against Guatemala on November 3. The wording of the letter was misleading, and made it sound as though the players and Federation had come to an agreement. A lot of the players who received the contracts were not regulars with the National Team and had no idea what was going on. When our lawyers asked the Federation who had been sent a contract, they wouldn't say. Most of the players, including the entire core group of National Team regulars, refused to accept the contract. We insisted that the Federation continue to negotiate with our lawyers.

The situation got worse when our lawyers filed an unfair labor practice complaint with the National Labor Relations Board in early October, alleging, among other things, that the Federation was wrongly refusing to negotiate with the players' collective bargaining agent. A week later, the Federation decided to send a "replacement" team to Peru. Some players who had been called in refused to go once they realized that the "real" team wasn't there. Others decided to go, thinking it might be their only chance with the National Team. The team that went ended up losing 4–1.

With the first World Cup qualifier only a few weeks away, the Federation was in disarray and the players were starting to wonder if we'd be playing against Guatemala. Fortunately, in the meantime, the Federation hired their own lawyers and that was when the negotiations got back on track, although they would drag on for another year. For the time being, we signed—under protest—the contracts the Federation originally sent us and played under the terms of those contracts while we waited for a decision from the NLRB.

The negotiations were difficult and created a fair amount of distance between the players and the Federation. The situation was a mess and wasn't to anyone's liking.

In the middle of all this, MLS began to experience its own legal problems when the newly-formed MLS Players Association filed a class action antitrust lawsuit against the league, challenging its "single-entity" status. There are business and legal advantages to a single-entity league, but from the players' perspective, the single-entity gave the league extraordinary control over player salaries, allocations, trades and transfers, marketing rights, and virtually everything else affecting a player's career. With the league minimum salary at $24,000 and the maximum at less than $200,000, and without any hope of free agency, the players began to talk early in 1996 about getting organized like players in other leagues. Two different groups wanted to represent us, the NFL Players

Association (which had represented the old NASL players) and an independent New York law firm.

As best I could tell, the NFLPA wanted us to form a players association, while the law firm wanted us to form a union. The legal specifics of each structure seemed to be beyond most of the players. One day, the D.C. United players voted overwhelmingly in favor of the law firm, and the next day voted 11–10 in favor of the NFLPA. No one seemed able to make up their mind. After at least two league-wide votes and a lot of confusion, the players sided with the NFLPA. I think the NFLPA won the second election by one vote, and that result was enough for them to declare themselves the players' representative. The law firm seemed to lose interest in fighting them on it, and that was that.

Since I was heavily involved with the National Team negotiations as captain and as a player rep, I stayed out of the MLS battle. All I really wanted was for us to take things slowly. The National Team players were in a strange position from the beginning, because most of us were making very good money compared to the majority of players in MLS. I wasn't for or against the NFLPA, but I did hear they were very aggressive. I was particularly worried that we would end up in court before any serious negotiation occurred with the league. That fear became a reality in February 1997 when the NFLPA filed its lawsuit.

The success of MLS is crucial to the future of soccer in the United States. But the players should be able to share in its prosperity. My biggest concern, and I wasn't the only one, was that all the legal proceedings and negotiations would drain the league's resources, create a huge debt for the players' association, distract from what was happening on the field, and maybe even kill the league altogether. I know the league isn't exactly making money hand over fist, and we have to proceed carefully on all fronts. But the league's first and foremost investment should be in its players. For now, unless there's a settlement out of court, the case looks like it's headed into the next century.

There's nothing quite like being pelted with ice—or AA batteries, in Alexi's case—walking off the pitch after a match, being spat on during a throw in, or having bags full of urine tossed on you when you go to take a corner kick. But that's what the National Team experienced when we went to San Jose, Costa Rica, during the first round of qualifying. Most Americans don't realize the conditions we're subjected to when we play out of the country, although this trip was more brutal than usual. We lost the match 2–1, but we survived the onslaught, spent a little extra time in the showers, and beat Costa Rica when they came to play us at Stanford two weeks later. That win assured us a spot in the final round of qualifying, but even though things were looking good for us, playing under Steve was changing.

Although Steve was criticized by the press and players after the U.S. team failed in the 1998 World Cup, the problems didn't arise all of a sudden. When he came on board as interim coach in 1995, the players took him for who he was and we liked the way he worked with us. We knew he didn't have a lot of experience, but he was always up front and honest about it. It's when he started to feel the pressure and began to overcoach that the situation got out of hand.

By the end of the first MLS season and the first round of qualifying for France in December 1996, things had already begun to deteriorate. Steve was barking at players in training and wasn't open to anything we had to say. Basically, he was turning into a control freak, and we weren't even under any serious pressure. In fact, the U.S. was never pressed during the first round of qualifying and we ended up clinching a spot in the next round early.

The first major U.S. tournament and warm-up for the final round of qualifying was the U.S. Cup in January. During the off-season, I had had a few years worth of bone spurs cleaned out of my ankle, so I didn't play. But, the truth is, the team that was there almost skipped the game against Mexico on January 19, because of continuing contract problems with the Federation. Once again, the night before a match the players weren't sure whether they would be playing. Nothing had been resolved after months of negotiations, and the players were still working under the contract that they'd signed under protest months earlier. Things were very tense. Within a month, we would win our complaint with the National Labor Relations Board, and that would give us better leverage in the negotiations. Regardless, arguing about contracts was not how we wanted to enter the final round of qualifying.

Even though I was unable to play, I went out to California to see the team's final game on my way to Hawaii with Cindi and Ian, for the first extended break I'd had in years. Before I got there, Steve told me over the phone that he was planning to give the younger guys an opportunity to play. He had been under pressure to do a better job of developing the younger players and the U.S. Cup was going to be his chance to experiment. The U.S. lost its first match to Peru 1–0, and then lost its second match to Mexico 2–0, after the near strike. When I arrived, Steve brought me up to his room to talk. He said that my leadership was needed and that he was glad I had come out for the last game because it showed my commitment to the team. It was painful to watch the team lose to Denmark 4–1, although it wasn't too surprising given how many new faces had been thrown together without much time to get organized. I was very surprised when I returned to my room after the match and found that Steve had left an urgent message for me to come speak with him as soon as I got in.

When I got to Steve's room, he asked me if I had known ahead of time about the meeting that had taken place after the game. I had no idea what he was talking about. "So you weren't aware?" he asked again. I was annoyed by the repetition and wondered why he was questioning me. He finally told me that, after the game, the younger players had been cleared out of the locker room, while the senior players remained behind to talk to him about everything from his lineup changes to the way he ran training. I said that I knew there had been complaints, but I didn't know that the players were planning to do this. I was surprised, actually. Steve said they told him that he'd changed, and he asked me if I thought he had changed, too. I was uneasy at that point, because I hadn't spoken with any of the guys. I told him, as tactfully as I could, that I thought he was different from the way he had been in 1995 and that the team had responded to him better back then. He didn't argue, didn't get mad, and told me he was glad that I hadn't known what was going on. I wasn't sure what that meant, really, but I felt as though he was questioning my integrity and my loyalty.

My first game of 1997 was our first final-round qualifying match, away against Jamaica in the beginning of March. I was still rehabbing my ankle and hadn't competed in a match yet. Steve and Assistant Coach Clive Charles said they knew that, but they couldn't stress enough how important it was that my leadership be on the field. It was an important game, we wanted to get the win, and they needed me to start. I let them know that I still wasn't at 100%, but Steve said that even 75% of John Harkes was good enough for him. I thought maybe I'd play for a half, but I was in for the full 90. We were tired, and I didn't feel sharp, and the conditions made matters worse. It was 95°, and we were playing on that hard, bouncy, Ping-Pong table that they call a field in Kingston. It made Gunnell Oval look like a golf green. The Reggae Boyz didn't lose a single first-round qualifying match at home. We left that game with a disappointing 0–0 tie, and no one was happy with the performance.

Our tie away to Jamaica was followed two weeks later by a match in Palo Alto against Canada. It wasn't expected to be a difficult game for us as a team, but it was a nightmare for me personally. The night before the game, I was invited to a barbecue at Christopher Sullivan's parents' house, in nearby Redwood City. I had remained good friends with Sully over the years and I hadn't seen his family or a while so I thought I would drop by for an hour. Unfortunately, the party had been catered and I ended up getting food poisoning—along with many other people.

I spent the entire night in the bathroom getting sick. It was horrible. I called the team doctor, Bert Mandelbaum, and he came to my room at 4:00, and again at 5:00 in the morning to see how I was doing. After his second visit, he advised me to set my alarm for 7:00 A.M. and come down to the training room so he could administer an IV to get some fluids back into my system. The food poisoning might be out of my system within 24 hours, but the risk of dehydration was there, and the game was at noon. My alarm went off and I got my IV, but I was completely drained and out of it. Steve was concerned, because he didn't think I would be able to play. I got to the stadium and Bert administered another IV before we went out to warm up. I felt good enough to play after warming up, and somehow made it through the first half. On my way into the tunnel at halftime, I saw Dr. Mandelbaum. All I said was, "Tell Steve I'm done."

I spent halftime in the bathroom, and assumed I would be subbed because I felt and looked like hell. While I was in there, the buzz of the locker room died down and I thought the team had gone back out to start the second half. I was right. But what I didn't realize at the time was that they were waiting for me and I was holding up the game. I heard Pam Perkins, the National Team Director, yell for me to get out on the field. She gave me a cup of tea and I ran out onto the pitch tucking in my shirt to join the rest of team. I couldn't believe it. I later found out that during the broadcast the TV commentators mentioned that I had food poisoning and had been on an IV, but the only people watching who knew what was *really* going on were Sully and his family—because they were suffering through the same thing! We were winning comfortably and eventually–and thankfully–I was subbed. We ended up winning 3–0.

It was nice to win, but it was expected, and our next match was away against Costa Rica on March 23. We hadn't forgotten how bad it was the last time we visited San Jose. But this time, after having been warned by FIFA about their treatment of us in December, the crowd was on their best behavior. We played well, but still lost 3–2, which was disappointing to everyone. The match was tied until the last minute, when we gave away a stupid goal. We could have walked away with a point, but instead Costa Rica got three and we left with none. We were critical of our own play, but also concerned with the way that Steve was handling things and constantly changing the lineup—three games into qualifying and we still weren't settled. Tony Sanneh had been thrown into the match after training with us for only a short time—a tough first cap.

Our next match was home against Mexico in Foxboro Stadium, Massachusetts. There was a lot of hype surrounding this match because of our fierce rivalry with Mexico and the fact that we were considered the top two teams in the qualifying run. It was also the first time that we would face our former coach, Bora. This also meant the match was important to Steve, because he wanted to show everyone that he was on par with his former boss. The fans, the players, the media—everyone wanted to see where the two teams stood. And we definitely wanted to beat Mexico at home, because we knew that beating them in Mexico City in the fall was going to be next to impossible.

The match was probably the most unpredictable we played during qualifying. It started out that way, at least. Just moments into the match, Mexico's Carlos Hermosillo, now with the L.A. Galaxy, blocked a Kasey Keller clearance with his face and sent the ball bouncing over Kasey's head into the net. I thought I was seeing things, but no one was as stunned as Kasey, and we had handed them a 1–0 lead while many fans were still finding their seats. Later, however, Mexico returned the favor, giving up an own goal. Both teams played hard, and the match ended 2–2, a fair result.

On June 29, we traveled down to San Salvador and the trip was a tense one. The State Department had issued a warning to Americans planning on attending the match, which was a complete overreaction and an insult to the Salvadoran fans. But it did keep some Americans away, and we were very thankful for the handful who showed up to watch. The game ended in a 1–1 tie, an unacceptable result. No disrespect to El Salvador, but we should have easily beaten that team, home or away. Steve had changed the lineup again, and that was unsettling. Players have to take responsibility for what happens on the field, but Steve was constantly tinkering and there didn't seem to be any clear rationale. As captain, I tried more than once to let Steve know that it was difficult to prepare for a match if you didn't know whether you were starting, where you were playing, and who you were playing alongside. After playing five out of ten final qualifying matches, we only had one win, and six points.

"I'm here fighting for every American coach," Steve would say in meetings when we were supposed to be talking about the next game. What Steve was fighting for was the chance to keep his job through the World Cup, and he only had through the end of qualifying to prove himself. But even though job pressure is there, a good coach won't show that to his players. It's a fact of life when you're a national team coach that you could lose your job at any time. To remind us of that was another sign of his lack of experience. We had enough to worry about once we got out on the field.

Steve's coaching techniques and constant fiddling earned him the title of "D. of T.": Director of Tactics. In meetings, he would stop the videotape and examine every little play. He was constantly stopping our training sessions to tell a player he needed to be five more yards this way or that, overanalyzing every move. He wouldn't just let us play. He had gone 180° from where he was two years earlier. He would tell Eric Wynalda how to hit a free kick, Joe-Max Moore how to hit a corner, or Preki how to swerve a ball. You've heard of micro-managing? Well, Steve was microcoaching. We tried to listen to him—he was the coach—but he was pointing out the obvious. Not having played professionally, let alone internationally, and without a successful coaching career behind him, Steve's book smarts lacked credibility to a group of guys who had hundreds and hundreds of caps among them. It had been said that the more he coached, the worse we got.

In training we would split into two groups, one going with Steve and the other going with Assistant Coach Clive Charles. He'd say things in that cockney accent of his like, "How many chances d'ya get to just play, boys? Let's have fun today." I would sometimes have a word with Clive when things got tense with Steve. He would talk with Steve on our behalf and things would change for a week or so, but then go back to normal. Looking back, maybe going to Clive so often was a mistake. As the situation with Steve went downhill, I wondered how Clive had represented the players' views to Steve—especially mine.

The players had July and August off from qualifying to spend time with their clubs. The chemistry at D.C. United was probably better than at most clubs because a lot of us had played for Bruce at UVA and already knew each other. We also didn't have a coaching change or any major lineup changes going into the second season, unlike a lot of other teams. As a result, D.C. was having an incredible season—we were virtually unstoppable. Without too many worries about my club team, my mind was on how the National Team was going to perform during the second half of qualifying.

The first week of September, we played Costa Rica at home in Portland and we needed a win to give ourselves some breathing room. I was unable to play because I had accumulated two yellow cards, and Waldo was out due to injury. But, after eight months of rehabbing his ACL, Tab was back. The almost entirely pro-American crowd in Portland

Tab, Preki, and I discussing a free kick during a World Cup qualifier.

was the best in recent memory, and we hoped the atmosphere would help get us a win. The first half came and went, and the game was scoreless. As the second half wore on, it looked like we would have to settle for a draw. But in the 78th minute, Preki crossed from the right, Marcelo laid a great

180

one-touch pass to Tab, and he let loose a spectacular shot from about 25 yards out that hit the back of the net.

At that point, we were closing in on qualifying for France and next up was a match against Jamaica at home in RFK. We were confident after our win against Costa Rica and were expecting to take three points from Jamaica, a team considered at the time to be much less threatening. I, along with Roy Wegerle, Jeff Agoos, and Eddie Pope, was also looking forward to playing in RFK, our D.C. United home field. We started the game playing a 3-5-2, not a formation we had much experience with. I remember discussing the formation with a few others. We thought it would be a mistake to change from a 4-4-2 and that we might have to waste a substitution too early in the game if the 3-5-2 wasn't working. That's exactly what happened. Steve substituted Jeff Agoos for Mike Sorber in the first half and we moved back to a 4-4-2.

A win would have meant a cakewalk to the end of qualifying. Instead, we tied and didn't look too good, particularly in the first half. We didn't really go after them like we should have. We gave away another bad goal on a mistake in the back, when Agoos tried to square the ball and it got picked off. Tying that game put us under a lot of pressure and we had to refocus. Qualifying for the World Cup came down to three games in November: away against Mexico and Canada, and at home against El Salvador. Rumors about Steve being fired were everywhere and the Federation wasn't backing him.

In preparation for the final stretch, the team trained in the mountains of Big Bear Lake, California, to adjust to the high-altitude we would have to deal with in Mexico City and to spend some time bonding. After D.C. United swept through the Eastern Conference playoffs for a second straight year, I was playing in my second MLS Cup, this time against the Colorado Rapids. As a result, I came into camp late, along with the other United and Rapids players. MLS Cup '97 was almost a repeat of the year before as far as the weather was concerned—pouring down rain, slippery conditions. This time, though, D.C. United was in control from the beginning, and while Colorado had had a great run through the playoffs, we won the match, 2–1. RKF was soldout, the crowd was fantastic, and the atmosphere was incredible notwithstanding the rain. After such a long season dividing time between qualifying matches and MLS games, it was a relief that United was able to pull off the championship. Again. Unfortunately, I didn't have much time to celebrate with the team or my family and had to leave immediately to join the team in California.

Big Bear was beautiful, and for that reason I was looking forward to it. But when I arrived, it was clear that the players who had been there were on edge. Everyone felt cooped up and was starting to go stir crazy. During our time at Big Bear, Steve introduced the "word of the day" in training. He would have us stand in a circle, holding hands, and players would take turns sharing their "word of the day" with the rest of the team. My first practice back, Steve asked me to offer that day's word. Now, no one had explained to me in advance what this was all about, so I hesitated, not sure whether Steve was kidding, and if not, what kind of word would be appropriate.

"Uhhh . . . ," I stuttered as I looked around the circle at players winking, smiling, and making other encouraging faces. "How about 'respect'? Has that been used?"

"Great word, Harkesy, Great word." Steve said, as a few players out of his sight nodded approvingly or gave me a thumbs up.

"Now . . . can you use it in a sentence?"

I don't remember my sentence, but it must have passed the test because there was a lot of "respect" on the practice field that day, then in the locker room, in our rooms, and during dinner. In the end, the "word of the day" generated a lot of laughs, especially when Frankie Hejduk asked if "dude" was OK, and Thomas Dooley—not a native English speaker—completely botched his sentence.

Things took a turn for the worse when Tab reinjured his knee and was sent home, but not before having a blowout with Steve about the way Steve was handling training. Tab

With Jeff Agoos and Richie Williams holding up the Rothenberg Trophy after MLS Cup '97.

Meeting President Clinton at the White House after the MLS Cup 1997.

had just come back and his getting injured again was almost as devastating to the team as it was to Tab. Ernie Stewart was injured, too, and Kasey Keller had torn his thumb playing for Leceister City in the English Premier League. It was one thing after another, everyone was tense, but trying to hold on because we were heading into the home stretch. Steve was leaning on me as captain even more.

Looking back, I wish I hadn't had so many meetings with Steve. He would always ask, "How are the players?" He wanted to know how they were feeling, what they were thinking, where their heads were. He put me under a lot of pressure during qualifying, especially with regard to Eric Wynalda, who performed at the highest level in games, but was not the best practice player. Steve would talk to me during training about Eric and tell me that he needed to work harder. "Go talk to him," he'd say. Whenever Eric lost his top,

184

in training or with the press, Steve would take me aside and say, "You need to sit down with him, you can get through to him." He also vented to me a lot about other players, and that wasn't fair to me because they were friends and colleagues, not to mention the fact that I wanted to focus on my own game. He would tell me which players were going to be criticized in the next team meeting and that I should tell them to be on their guard. Steve wanted me to be his messenger and that undermined my role as captain because it separated me from the other players and made me look like Steve's assistant, rather than a peer. He should have had more conversations with players one-on-one, behind closed doors, including with me.

On November 2, we went down to Mexico City to play in one of the most intimidating stadiums in the world. The United States had never gotten a result in Mexico, and we knew getting one in qualifying was going to be nearly impossible. There were 110,000 Mexicans screaming at us through the heat, smog, and thin air of Azteca. It's an amazing stadium, and all soccer fans should try to experience a game there at least once in their lives. A lot of families had traveled down for this game, including Cindi and our six-month-old baby, Lauren. Lauren stayed in the hotel with a baby-sitter while Cindi went to the game, because we knew the atmosphere inside the stadium was going to be intense. It's a good thing Lauren stayed behind, because unfortunately the tickets for the families were in the general admission seats behind the goal—they were basically thrown to the lions. They ended up getting pelted with eggs before the game. Thank God the players didn't find out about this until afterward, or else we would never have been able to concentrate.

Everything was against us from the start—as it is for any team that steps onto that field—and then, to make matters worse, Jeff Agoos got red-carded in the first half and we had to play a man down. I moved to left back and helped shut down Mexican forward Luis Hernandez. By midway through the second half, with the game still tied 0–0, we had turned the crowd against their own team. They shouted *"Olé!"* after every pass we completed and were calling for Bora to be fired. We walked away from the game with a tie and a qualifying point, thank you very much. Spirits were high.

We got back to the hotel, and I spent some time hanging out in the lobby. Cindi and I showed off Lauren to my teammates, as most new parents do. We had dinner with a few players and then I took Cindi and Lauren back to the family hotel before turning in. I was happy: when the chips were down, our team had come up big once again.

The next morning, Roy Wegerle and I didn't get our wake-up call—unless, of course, you consider someone speaking broken English and banging on the door saying that the team had just left to be a wake-up call. We grabbed our stuff, jumped in a taxi, and rushed to the airport, but no one was there. The team hadn't left, the bus had been parked on the side of the hotel, and we had beaten them to the airport. When they arrived, Roy and I were sitting at the gate, drinking coffee, and reading the paper. I found out later that Tom King, the team's general manager, had called Cindi's hotel room looking for me, but didn't knock on our door. Roy and I were fined $100 each for missing the bus. It wasn't enough to worry about, but we weren't too happy. Somehow we had become responsible for a mixed-up wake-up call.

A week later, we clinched our spot in France with a game to spare, beating Canada 3–0 in Vancouver. The champagne was flowing in the locker room and, after nearly two years of qualifying, going to France was finally a reality. Everyone was so relieved—an enormous weight had been lifted. We called Tab from the locker room after the game. Steve walked up to me, gave me a hug, and said, "We did it! You're going to your third World Cup."

At the time, I believed him.

Our final qualifying match was against El Salvador at Foxboro. For us, it was an opportunity to close the gap between ourselves and Mexico in the qualifying standings and put on a good show for our fans. But for El Salvador it was a chance to go to the World Cup. Roy and I received a phone call in our room offering us money if we would throw the game. I didn't know who it was so I wasn't too worried about it. Afterward, the Federation put a number of security measures in place. That's how much it meant to El Salvador. But we were playing for pride, and after tying El Salvador in the previous match, we wanted the win. Steve could afford to move things around, and in that game used me as an attacking midfielder. The team played well, we won 4–2, I notched two assists, and the team finished qualification just one point behind Mexico.

The Federation waited until December to tell Steve the job was his through the World Cup, even though we had qualified midway through November. Everyone knew that Alan Rothenberg hadn't made up his mind about Steve. The Federation also knew that the players were not happy, and the press had criticized the way we'd qualified—struggling when we shouldn't have. I wrote in my column on ESPN's website that I thought Steve should get to keep his job because he had coached us through qualifying and had earned the right to be there. As players, we didn't always agree with his tactics and coaching techniques, but we thought it was too late to have someone new come in and, everything else being equal, we preferred an American coach. So we gave Steve the benefit of the doubt and Steve helped himself by being a good politician and playing up to the press. He claimed that he didn't like to criticize players in the media, and always insisted to us that we keep team problems private. But he purposefully used the media to put pressure on players like Lexi, Marcelo, and Eric. And in the months leading up to the World Cup, Steve would use the press against me. The team thought that once the job was his, he would relax and things would be better. We couldn't have been more wrong.

During the MLS off-season, I talked with Bruce and D.C. United General Manager, Kevin Payne, about my role at the club. New England Revolution Coach Thomas Rongen, who occasionally worked with the National Team and had expressed interest in me a few months earlier at the MLS All-

Star game, was wondering whether I would consider leaving D.C. for Boston. I respected Rongen and considered his interest a great compliment, especially after he said he would like to build the team around me. That got my attention because I knew it would add some spark to my game going into the World Cup. On the other hand, the idea of uprooting my family and leaving a winning club and good organization was not too appealing. Bruce and Kevin assured me that they wanted me to stay and explained the role they saw for me in the coming season. Among other things, Bruce hinted that he thought it would be better if Marco Etcheverry, our attacking midfielder, took over as captain, because I was expected to be in and out of town with the National Team and he needed a captain who would be there full-time. I understood that and let them know shortly afterward that I really wanted to stay at D.C. As reported in the press, the issue dragged on for another two months, because the MLS league office decided to get tough with the salary cap rules and determined that D.C. United was over the $1.3 million limit. Something had to be done, but it took a while for things to get sorted out.

In the meantime, the National Team reported to camp in Orlando, Florida, in the beginning of January. We had drawn Germany, Yugoslavia, and Iran in the first round of the World Cup, which was not only a very difficult group, but also the most politically charged. There was a lot of work to do between January and June. Between friendlies and the CONCACAF Gold Cup tournament, we were basically going to be away from home for about two months straight. Steve brought in a large pool of players, some who had been with us throughout qualifying, others who had not.

Steve and I had a meeting soon after the team arrived in camp to talk about where the team stood, going into the final phase of preparation for the World Cup: players' strengths and weaknesses, lineup options, etc. Looking at a diagram of the field, he asked me where I saw myself playing. He pointed toward the middle of the field, and I nodded in agreement. Then he said, "You could also play in back."

"Yeah, Steve, I guess I can play anywhere."

188

"But I see you . . . " he said, followed by a dramatic "Steve" pause, "here or here," and pointed to left midfield and center midfield. That was fine with me. He also asked if I would consider playing defensive midfield. I said, "Sure."

As I was getting ready to leave, Steve talked about how much we had been through together, and then added that Alan Rothenberg was not a big fan of either of us. I asked if it was because of the role I had played in the contract negotiations. Steve said he didn't really know why, but that he had defended me. He made it sound like he wanted to protect me. He said we needed to stick together.

During camp, it was clear that time off and new job security had not mellowed Steve. He continually put down MLS while he bent over backward for guys coming over from Europe. How could he take digs at the MLS, a league we all came back for and helped build? It was the league *he* had promoted, too, saying he wanted us here because he would have more access to his pool of players. When Steve sent Peter Vermes and Mike Sorber home from camp, he had a team administrator tell them, rather than telling them himself. He cut Mark Chung during practice one day without Mark knowing that the entire conversation was being taped for ESPN and would be aired nationally in June.

At that point, I was edgy because I still wasn't sure which MLS club I would be playing with in the coming season. Then, on January 7, I was told that Ron Atkinson, who was back managing at Sheffield, was interested in bringing me over. It sounded like a great opportunity, playing back in the Premier League, helping Sheffield avoid relegation, and getting sharp for the World Cup. But Sheffield wanted me on loan only, and the league wouldn't hear of it. When the trade with New England didn't go through either, I was happy to stay a member of D.C. United. I'd always liked United—that was never an issue—the players and the club, so it looked like things had worked out for the best and it was nice to know where my family and I were going to be. Our month-long camp with the National Team finally came to an end, and we finished it off with a friendly against Sweden, which we won 1–0.

February was the CONCACAF Gold Cup, our biggest tournament before the World Cup. Steve wanted us to play quicker than we needed to. The players knew that Cuba, for example, was not a strong side and thought that we should have slowed things down at times and not forced the play. You need to pick your spots. You don't go 100 mph and wear out your team early on in a tournament if you don't have to. But we couldn't say anything. Things had to be done Steve's way or else, he'd say, "You'll be . . . *there*," and motion toward the bench, making one of his many hand gestures.

By the second week of February, the boys were starting to get tired, but somehow we managed to pull off one of the greatest upsets in U.S. soccer history: a 1–0 victory over Brazil in the L.A. Coliseum. The U.S. had never even tied Brazil, let alone beaten them. And the last three times we'd played them we'd lost 1–0: 1996 in L.A., 1995 at Copa America, and 1994 during the World Cup. No one was expecting those results to be reversed that night. But once the game got started, we were right there with them. They had numerous chances to score in the first half, but we held on, and in the second half we started to create opportunities in their half of the field. Shortly after coming on as a sub in the second half, Preki scored the lone U.S. goal. It felt like we had won the World Cup. We knew if we could hold on to that lead we would be making history. And we did, thanks in large part to Kasey Keller—nothing got by him. The man was a wall. He frustrated the hell out of Romario, the Brazilian striker, who told the press after the game that it was the best performance he'd ever seen from a goalkeeper. There may have been only about 12,000 people on hand to see it, but everybody all over the world heard about it. It was a thrill and an honor to be on the field with my teammates for that once-in-a-lifetime experience.

After coming off such a huge win, it was a big disappointment to lose the final to Mexico, a team we'd beaten in the past and had recently tied on their own turf. It was a significant accomplishment to be playing in the final of a tournament as important as the CONCACAF Gold Cup, in front of a full house, but the crowd was the worst I've ever experienced in the United States. They booed during the National Anthem, and yelled obscenities at our players. As an American soccer player, you're often in a situation where you don't have a "home" crowd for home games, but it doesn't help when matches are scheduled against Mexico in L.A. Whether the Federation or CONCACAF is responsible, I don't know, but *we* have to play a tournament final as the "visiting" team. It may not be unusual, but you never get used to it.

The press had been questioning Steve about who would play defensive midfield and, throughout the Gold Cup, Steve used me there. I never asked to play there, but was willing to do what was best for the team. For close to a year, I had spent most of my time playing left midfield. But when he needed to, Steve used me as a utility player, and told me he wanted me to play wherever I could to help the team. After the Gold Cup, Steve criticized me for being inconsistent. Maybe I didn't play my best. But like all the veteran players, I was focused on the World Cup and hoped to be on form in June, not February. And if Steve didn't think I was pulling my weight, he could have put me on the bench. Instead, I started every game of the tournament and the next two friendlies before the team's first break in nearly two months.

Following the Gold Cup, we flew to Miami, got off the plane, changed into our gear, and trained for an hour in preparation for our upcoming friendly against Holland. My ankle was sore, so I got an X-ray and discovered I had a bone chip floating around in there. During training the next day, Steve asked me if I was fit. If I wasn't, he said he had other guys coming in for the game that he needed to look at. I waited to see what he'd say next. I was thinking, "If you want me to sit, tell me to sit." But he could never come right out and tell me things. He told me there were three possible scenarios. One: I play left midfield. Two: I play central midfield. Three: I don't play at all. I told him I wanted to play. Of course, as a player, you want to play every game.

One of the greatest upsets in U.S. soccer history: a 1–0 victory over Brazil.

The day before the game, he put up the starting lineup before training and I wasn't on it. Guys were asking me throughout training what was going on and I told them I didn't know. Then Steve came walking over to me toward the end of training, as I was crossing balls to the strikers, and said, "You're going to play left back for me tomorrow." I had a ball at my feet, looked up for a minute, crossed it to one of the forwards and said, "Fine Steve, whatever."

"You got a problem with that?"

I said, "No," but I knew then that he was looking to pick a fight.

I told him I was confused because none of the scenarios he had presented to me included playing left back. Once again, he hadn't come out and said what he was thinking.

"Are you calling me a liar?"

I stared at him then, and couldn't believe he was getting so upset. "Slow down, Steve. That's not what I said." But I knew he wasn't hearing me.

We went back to the hotel for lunch, and on our way to the team meeting I pulled Steve aside and said, "Steve, I want to apologize for what happened out on the field."

"I accept your apology," he said and, after a pause added, "But I'm still pissed off."

"Steve, you know I never meant to piss you off. We got our lines crossed. You know I'll play anywhere for the team."

"It's good to hear that," he said. And we continued on to the meeting.

Eddie Pope was injured so I played in back against Holland, and we lost 2–0. I played OK considering we were playing a team as good as Holland; a lot of guys had been moved around and the whole team was starting to get tired from all the games and travel. Actually, I consider my versatility to be one of my strengths, but it's difficult for any player to step into a new position and play well, especially against a team that would go on to the semifinals of the 1998 World Cup.

We left the night of the Holland match for a friendly against Belgium in Brussels and I said goodbye to Cindi, who had come down to the game to see me off. I knew being on her own for nearly two months with two small children was tough and I told her to hang in there. As players, we were physically and mentally exhausted. We had played many international games in a short period of time, traveling from coast to coast and now across the Atlantic. We missed our families and had eaten too much hotel food. No one felt they knew where they stood with Steve and communication was nonexistent. I tried to relay to Steve whenever possible how the guys were feeling and that he should open up a bit. Steve was not a people person. He thought that more discipline and forced togetherness was the way to fix things, when in truth what was needed, in my view, was a short break to refresh ourselves. But I don't think he appreciated that I was trying to improve morale. The day after we arrived, we traveled an hour and a half so that we could train at a Nike complex. Europe is six hours ahead, so training took place at what our bodies thought was around sunrise—after playing a full 90 minutes and traveling for eight hours the night before.

I was rooming with Joe-Max Moore in Belgium, and it was his birthday. He was injured, we were all stressed, and it was two nights before the game. So a group of players decided to go out to celebrate Joe's birthday. We had been through hell and needed a break, and it was the most relaxed we'd been in weeks. Unfortunately, Joe got sick, so Eric and I took him back to the hotel fairly late, got him up to our room, and put him in bed. The rest of the crowd came in shortly after. Maybe it wasn't the best idea, but the guys needed to get out and be together.

We lost the Belgium game, 2–0. Belgium ran at us hard, but didn't play particularly well. We had a lot of chances that we just didn't put away. I played defensive midfield the entire game and if Steve wasn't pleased with my performance against Holland or Belgium, he didn't say anything to me. We weren't happy with the result, but we were ecstatic to be going home. Steve never said a word to me about our night out, although I learned later that he did speak to both Eric and Joe-Max about it.

A couple weeks after the Belgium match, Steve was on

his way to Germany to watch the German National Team play Brazil. Steve had stated to the press that he would be naming at least 10 players to the World Cup squad within the next few weeks and was in the process of meeting with all regular members of the National Team player pool to let them know where they stood. I was expecting to be named as one of those ten. On his way to Germany he stopped to meet with the players based in D.C. He rented a conference room in a hotel about 10 minutes from United's training ground.

When I arrived for my meeting, he was very cold. He poured me a glass of water and sat down. "Well I'll come straight to the point. I'm not sure about taking you to the World Cup. Well, let's backtrack. I'm not taking you to Austria."

I waited for the punch line. A chuckle. Anything.

But I could see that Steve wasn't kidding and that he was really angry, so I decided the best thing was to give him the floor and let him vent.

"For months it's been one thing after another with you," he said. "And now I find out about this Belgium thing." He started to go into great detail about a conversation he had had with a security guard at our hotel in Belgium. I let him keep going.

"As captain, you should have walked away from that situation."

I waited for what was coming next.

"Then there's the Holland situation . . . " he said.

I thought we had settled that. It took everything I had not to lash out, but I knew that would be a mistake. I didn't know how long I could hold on.

"You missed flights with Eric and Roy, and you and Roy missed the bus to the airport in Mexico City." Steve knew what had happened in both those instances, but I still said nothing.

"You've got to be the first in meetings, the first on the bus. Not the last. You're setting bad examples. I need you to change." Finally, he seemed to be taking a breath.

"Can I say something now?" I asked. And I tried to give my explanations as calmly as possible.

My biggest fans—Lauren and Ian Harkes.

I explained that, as far as Belgium was concerned, no harm had been done. I didn't understand why he hadn't said anything sooner, especially since he had spoken to Eric and Joe-Max two weeks earlier. If anything, that night out brought us together. Guys were so depressed by that point that, if anything, it helped us unwind and prepare for the game. I thought it was better to help out, not walk away. Steve had blown things out of proportion—although I didn't tell him that—and it showed that he had little feel for team chemistry. But I apologized for the night out, and added that it was no reason to keep me off the Austria trip.

In response to our confrontation before the Holland game, I told him, "I already apologized to you for that, Steve. But you said I called you a liar. I did not."

I moved on to the next topic, and said that although Eric and I took a later flight one morning after a match, we did so because we didn't have training that day. Roy and I didn't miss a flight, we missed a connection in Dallas because of a time change. We were sitting across from our gate eating in TGIFridays when the plane took off. Stupid, sure, but not blatant disrespect for anyone's schedule. It's not like we wanted to sit in the airport for another three hours, and we didn't miss any training. But when I thought about the flights, the bus, and the night out, and thought of all the other people involved, what I really wanted to say was, "OK, now there's a double standard?"

But I wasn't about to raise that issue. What really got me were Steve's comments about my setting bad examples. I played in 13 out of 16 qualifiers and finished qualifying with the most assists on the team. Setting a good example as captain is not making sure you're first into a room for a meeting. A captain is a guy who puts his heart out on the field for the team, no matter what. A captain pushes himself and will lift up a guy when he's down. He's not a Boy Scout and he's not a coach's mouthpiece, because then his teammates lose respect for him.

"Steve, I'm sorry if maybe I didn't handle things in the best way at all times. We were under a lot of pressure, both of us, especially during qualifying. But I don't think it's a reason to leave me off the team. I have changed and I hope you'll give me the chance to prove that."

"I can see that you've changed. It shows in your play. D.C. is reaping the benefits of you as a player right now. But this is what I'm planning to do."

At that point, Steve was calmer, but he still wasn't finished.

"This decision hasn't been easy," Steve said. "One day you'll be sitting here making these decisions and I will support that." I felt like he was waiting for me to respond, but I didn't know what to say to that.

He finished up by saying, "Let's leave this for now." He told me the door was open and that I should feel free to call him.

I wondered where this anger had come from. Steve had never said a word to me. Clive had never said anything like, "Watch it, Harkesy—He's gonna blow up at you." Nothing. I was very calm about the whole thing, probably because I was so shocked. If he had a problem with me, why hadn't he disciplined me? He could have benched me, taken my captaincy away or, better yet, come right out and told me.

I left the meeting thinking he was testing me, as he had Eric, Preki, and Frankie, all of whom had either been benched or left off trips to prove a point and then brought back when he thought they had learned their lesson. But I didn't know why he would do it so close to the World Cup. I sat in my car for 15 minutes and wondered what had happened between starting at central midfield as captain in Belgium and sitting in the Hyatt parking lot watching my international career flash before my eyes.

Other than before the Holland game, I never had what I considered a serious confrontation with Steve. Maybe Steve thought we did, but if that's true, he was far too subtle for a kid from Kearny. That's not to say that Steve and I were close; he wasn't close to anyone. But I thought we got along well enough, even if I did speak my mind on occasion, but even then only when players were coming to me with complaints and it seemed necessary for team morale to say something. Steve too often took my comments as if they were coming from me, and only me, rather than from the team as a whole. Perhaps that was his mechanism for denying there were problems.

I got home and Cindi asked me how the meeting went. I knew the last thing she was expecting was what I was about to tell her.

"Not very good, not good at all . . . " and I was having a hard time getting it all out.

"In fact, I'm not going to Austria. He even threatened me with not going to the World Cup."

We talked for a while, and Cindi did her best to calm me down. Later that night, I walked over to Bruce's house. He told me that he and Kevin Payne had met with Steve the night before.

"I kinda had a feeling this was going to happen," Bruce said, and added that he sensed a lot of Steve's insecurities with regard to me. Bruce and Kevin had made a point of telling Steve what a good season I was having, and that when they had problems with me, they talked to me about it and I made the changes that were necessary. Bruce told Steve that after we'd had our off-season talk, I was the player they needed me to be: totally committed, focused, and there for the team.

I was disappointed that Bruce and Kevin knew Steve was going to come down on me, and hadn't warned me. But they had told him to settle down. Bruce's advice to me was to bite my tongue and wait it out. Things would calm down.

I was a mess all week in training. I felt sick and numb and wasn't sleeping. But I wasn't about to tell anyone what had happened. I was waiting to talk to Steve again and see if things would blow over. Roy Wegerle came up to me at practice the day after my meeting and said Steve had warned him about the meeting he was going to have with me. I was furious that he had discussed my situation with another player. At that point, I didn't know what to think about anything.

I called Steve a week later when he got back from Germany. He was keeping the door and phone lines open, so he said, which made me feel a little better. I knew the Austria roster would be announced soon. The night before the teleconference to announce the team for that match, I called Clive Charles and asked him to be straight with me and tell me what was going on.

All he said was, "I don't know what to tell you, Harkesy. I'm shocked as well."

He added that it was smart not to talk to the press. "We've just got to get you back on that plane, son." He also said he didn't think Steve knew how to handle me. He told me to sit tight, things would settle down.

found out I wasn't going to the World Cup on a conference call.

I thought I would be left off the Austria trip, but I wanted to listen in on the teleconference announcing the roster anyway. So after training, I went into Bruce's office with him and we called in. That's when Steve announced to the press that he was not only leaving me off the Austria roster, but not currently planning to bring me to France, either.

I stared at Bruce's phone. I couldn't believe he hadn't discussed it with me first, or at least called to let me know. As shocked reporters asked him about the decision, he became defensive, got off track, and started pulling justifications out of the air—some of which I'd never heard before.

I didn't "embrace" the left back position, Steve said, and I knew he was talking about our confrontation before the Holland match. Then he said that I had a strong personality that held Claudio Reyna back on the field. What?! How insulting is that to Claudio? Steve said he was now building the team around Claudio, and that meant Chad Deering, Claudio's teammate in Germany, would get first shot at the supporting defensive midfield position. When reporters on the call brought up the fact that Chad wasn't even playing regularly for his club team, Wolfsburg, Steve said Chad was being punished for leaving to come play National Team games for the U.S. At that point, Dave Sarachan, our assistant coach, and Bruce's former assistant at UVA, poked his head into Bruce's office and said, "How's that possible? He's had more than one coach over there. Each one has punished him for the same reason?" No one bothered to point out that Chad had only played one game for the U.S., and that was only recently. I was also wondering why none of these things had been mentioned to me. Steve was really reaching and, at least to players and other people in the know, further undermining his credibility.

Steve then added that there were "leadership concerns" that would remain private, as if he were showing this incredible amount of respect for our relationship. I wondered what the hell he was referring to—the planes, the bus, Belgium?—but I had no idea at the time how much trauma that one comment would cause me.

The call ended and Bruce didn't know what to say to me. I was devastated. I walked out of his office, down the hall, and Ken Meese of local Channel 9 was in the lobby. The last thing I wanted to do right then was an interview, but I had nothing to hide, so I talked to him. I took the high road and didn't blow my top. That would have been the easy thing to do. I told Ken that I was upset and disappointed, but that Steve was the coach and I had to respect his decision. Ken then asked whether Steve's decision meant the end of my international career, and I responded that Steve had left the door open for my return and I hoped he meant it. People say that I handled the situation with dignity and class, but deep down I wanted to lash out, or at least tell people that Steve had not, in fact, told me in our earlier meeting that he would not be taking me to the World Cup. That was untrue and it made me look dishonest to the various sponsors who had spent thousands of dollars developing World Cup promotions with me as the centerpiece.

I got home and told Cindi what had happened. She was stunned and couldn't believe that an already horrible situation had managed to get worse. My father called shortly after that. "This man has made a decision and it's a bad one," he said to me. "But you just keep your mouth shut, ride this out, and you will rise above it." I talked to Rob McCourt and my close friends in Kearny. As always, they supported me and were there for me. No questions asked.

I tried to make sense of what had happened, but it wasn't easy. Cutting me was Steve's way of saying, "I'm making my mark. I'm cutting my captain." It was the strongest message he could have possibly sent to anyone on the team who was thinking about questioning his authority. I'd gone from being Steve's message boy to being the message itself. And in the process, he tried to bury me. That's what angered me the most: the way he handled it left so many doubts in people's minds, it was completely irresponsible.

Thomas Dooley would be Steve's new captain after the press had written, time after time, that Steve had called me his "captain for life." Steve denies ever saying that—he never said it directly to me—and I never took the title seriously anyway, knowing like everything else in soccer that the title was temporary and that the job was mine only for as long as I deserved it. Still, after all the times it had been seen in print, it made my dismissal even more shocking to some.

Thomas called me the very next morning and said he couldn't believe what Steve had done. Claudio called too, and left several long messages on my machine. He was very upset and angry that Steve had involved him at all. He wanted to make sure I knew that he had never said anything about me to Steve. Hank Steinbrecher called and wanted to let me know that there were still many opportunities to work with the Federation. Sunil Gulati called and said he didn't know what to tell me.

Actually, it seemed like the only person I didn't hear from was Steve. I left a message for him the day after, but he didn't call back. He had left for England the next morning and was unavailable for comment. So the press converged on me, and I continued to take the high road.

Sunil came to D.C. that Friday and met with Cindi and

Running through the midfield in World Cup qualifier.

me. He was very supportive, but didn't give me any of the answers I was looking for. I looked at Sunil as a man with considerable power in the Federation, who knew that Steve's job had been on the line ever since he'd gotten it, and he was telling me that the Federation couldn't do anything. It was "Steve's team." I understood that on some level, but when I thought back on the comments that Alan Rothenberg made in the press, and how the Federation was always on the lookout for a replacement, I couldn't believe that they were letting him get away with this after I had spent 11 years with the National Team. More importantly, I couldn't believe they were allowing him to handle it so poorly, calling my character into question in the process. That was something the Federation could control as Steve's and my employer.

Sunil said all he could really do was try to arrange a meeting between Steve and me. He said then, and in following conversations, that a flight to L.A. would show Steve how much being on the team meant to me. I felt like I was in the middle of one big chess game trying to guess Steve's next move. All the while the bait—getting back on the team—was being dangled in front of my nose. I was shattered. Cindi, who had been so strong up to that point, broke down in tears.

The only thing that kept me going was my family and friends. But not knowing what my future was with the National Team and having my name attacked in the press put me through hell every day.

Tab called me two nights before the Austria game and got me all wound up again. Steve had been taking shots at me in the press and Tab couldn't understand why I wasn't striking back. But I would do whatever it took to get to the World Cup. I kept mum. I didn't want to give Steve any ammunition to say anything about my attitude. The night before the Austria game Ron Atkinson called to tell me that he was still interested in getting me to Sheffield at some point. Lexi called too, at about 4:00 A.M. Austria time. It was a confidence boost to receive such support. Steve had had a meeting with the players to tell them why he had cut me. He mentioned the planes, buses, Belgium, playing left back, told them I had called him a liar, and made a reference to other mysterious leadership issues. He also told them that there would be no group discussion of his decision. If players wanted to, they could speak to him individually. Those "leadership issues that will remain private between John and me," as Steve said, were never discussed with me. Ever.

I watched the U.S.-Austria game at D.C. United. I thought Austria was average and that the 3-6-1 would be shaky against Germany. But the U.S. won 3–0, and that result changed the course of U.S. soccer history. It was good that the U.S. won, but I don't know what kind of coach bases a team and a formation on one result, or bases a player's spot on the National Team on one performance. But Steve did. What happens game in and game out should determine a team. But every decision Steve had made up to that point—cutting me, changing the formation, building around a single player—was justified by that one result. And it was lucky for him, because more than one person told me that if the U.S. hadn't won, there was a replacement in line. I was still holding out hope for a spot, but it didn't look likely under the circumstances.

After not returning any of my calls, and under pressure from Sunil, Steve finally agreed to have a meeting with me and my U.S. agent, Craig Sharon, who began representing me shortly after I came back from England. We flew out to L.A. on May 4, the day before Steve was going to announce most of his roster for the World Cup. I knew it was my last shot.

Steve wanted Bert Mandelbaum, the team doctor, to be there too, and we met at Mandelbaum's office. It was kind of a weird setting and there were still some patients filtering out when Craig and I arrived. Steve got there and I didn't say much. I didn't shake his hand. I couldn't. Luckily, Craig broke the ice. Going in, I was definitely expecting the worst.

For about 45 minutes, Steve and I discussed the same old story—the planes, the bus, Belgium, etc.—and basically had the same conversation we'd had six weeks earlier when he said I wasn't going to Austria. Steve said that there was no one incident that led to his decision and that the problem had developed over time—an accumulation of things. We still disagreed about whether or not I had called Steve a liar before the Holland game.

"I'll admit you did not use those words," he said. "But that's what I thought you meant."

I was so frustrated, I didn't know how to respond.

Once Steve and I finished rehashing what we'd already gone through in my first meeting, I told him that he should give me a chance. I said I didn't need a captain's armband to be a leader on the team.

"You can't tell me I'm not one of the top 22 players in the country, Steve."

"This has nothing to do with your ability," Steve said, and he started to go on and on about how I was on fire with United and how they were reaping the benefits of me as a player. "But," he added, "can you be that leader for me? I have a lot of kids on the team who need discipline. I know your ability, but can you be that leader?"

Steve said that a few players on the team had a problem with me, but he wouldn't tell me who. If there was a communication breakdown, between me and Steve or between me and a player, Steve or the player should have talked to me. To my knowledge, I've never had a problem with any player during the 11 years that I've played for the National Team. And during my time with the National Team, the group of guys that went through qualifying together were the closest I'd ever played with. It was a relief to finally be able to say to Steve what I couldn't say to the press.

When it looked like Steve and I had run out of things to say, Craig asked, "Is that it? Are those the reasons? There's nothing else?"

Steve said that was it.

Then Craig calmly shredded Steve's arguments.

"Even if we accept everything you've said at face value, it's not nearly enough to justify dropping John from the team after he has played nearly every minute of every game he has been available—as captain no less—for the past three years," Craig said, and talked about the contributions I'd made to the team and the relative insignificance of the alleged infractions, especially since in every case at least one other player was involved.

Craig admitted that I could have handled things better, but told Steve, "This situation is as much about what you didn't do as what John might have done."

"First, you didn't let John know how concerned you were about his behavior, which is particularly inexcusable if, in fact, the problem developed over time. You had ample time and opportunity to take an intermediate disciplinary step, but you elected to do nothing. Then when you finally decided to act, you imposed the 'death penalty,' hardly a fair first punishment."

"Second, you didn't treat John the same way that you treated other players. Eric was benched for not 'embracing' a new position, Alexi was benched for poor play, Preki was temporarily dropped for having a bad attitude, and Frankie Hejduk was temporarily dropped for missing a plane. Why was John treated so severely?"

"And third, you didn't test your assumption that John would be disruptive to the team if stripped of his captaincy or sat on the bench. Why make that assumption? Since D.C. United took away John's captaincy, he has played the best soccer of his MLS career."

Steve didn't disagree. "Maybe I should have been more of a bastard," he said. "But I didn't have a president who supported me." He also admitted that he had treated me differently from other players, taking a "hands-off" approach where I was concerned, hoping I would "come around on my own," whatever that meant.

After having the opportunity to speak my mind, I had settled down a bit. But this got me angry again. Craig responded to Steve's second point, making an analogy between the player-coach relationship and the parent-child relationship.

"If a father elects not to discipline his child, and instead lets the child learn from his own mistakes, and then down the road decides his hands-off approach isn't working, the father shouldn't just kick the child out of the house. Instead, he should tell the child that the rules have changed, if he doesn't like the new rules, he can leave, and that if he doesn't change, then he will be forced to leave." Unfortunately, Steve had acted like the parent who throws his kid out of the house without warning.

Steve had no argument.

Dr. Mandelbaum finally spoke up, in defense of Steve. "It sounds to me, in general, like a broken relationship. Steve no longer trusts John and wasn't getting what he needed from him as captain, so he decided to end the relationship."

"That's right! That's exactly it," Steve said, like a light-bulb had just gone off. That comment started to surface over and over in the papers.

Then Craig came through again with another perfect analogy. To Mandelbaum he said, "Imagine you're a marriage counselor, and a couple comes to you for advice, sits down, and the first thing the husband says is, 'I want a divorce.' The wife looks at the husband, shocked, and tells him that she had no idea things were so bad. 'Why haven't you told me?' she asks. Now, would you advise the husband to go ahead with the divorce, or would you tell the couple to try and work it out now that each spouse knows how the other feels?"

Of course, Bert said he would advise them to work it out. Apparently, that answer gave him new perspective, because he then asked if this meeting was an airing-out session or a problem-solving session. As if on cue, we all slowly turned and looked at Steve. Steve paused and said, much to my relief, "I consider it a problem-solving session."

I thought things were looking up.

Finally, Craig turned to the issue that had caused me so much anguish, "Setting aside the merits of Steve's decision, the announcement of John's dismissal couldn't have been handled any worse."

Steve's vague "leadership" references, combined with the fact that the announcement caught everyone so off guard, led people to believe that something scandalous *must* have happened. That caused rumors to fly. I heard everything: I had punched Steve in practice. I was having an affair with Steve's wife. I was having an affair with Eric's wife. I was on drugs. You name it. I looked Steve in the eye and told him that he knew the rumors were a lie. Steve said he was sorry that the rumors had started, but he didn't really take responsibility. Instead, he said that he couldn't control what people said, in a "you know how people can be" kind of way. Steve will never understand what his mishandling of my situation put Cindi and me through.

Steve finished up by saying that he would name 20 players to the roster the following day on ESPN, leaving two spots open. He said he would consider me as an alternate, although he would not list me as one, and that he would consider bringing me into camp two weeks later. When he said that, I felt like we'd made some real progress. Bert walked us out, shook my hand, and said, "I think this will all turn out OK." Craig and I got in the car and sat there. We thought it went surprisingly well.

But I gave Steve too much credit and that gave me hope.

The next day, Steve took a much tougher public stance on ESPN than he had with me in private, just as he did after we met in D.C. when he announced the roster for the Austria game. ESPN asked him point-blank about the possibility of my being one of the final roster additions, and Steve said it was highly unlikely and didn't mention that he was considering bringing me into camp. Twenty-four hours earlier he was asking me if I could be a leader for the younger players and suddenly it was as though the conversation never took place. It was a familiar Steve tactic: he can't handle confrontation, so he takes it easy on you in private and then rips you in front of the press when he knows he won't be seriously challenged.

In May, the U.S. played Kuwait and Macedonia as warm-ups for the biggest tournament in the soccer world. Not the toughest opponents. A month before the World Cup, teams really need to be tested. The U.S. should have been playing teams of a much higher quality. I continued to keep quiet with the media, but it was getting more difficult and the press was digging hard. I didn't want to disrupt things for the team any further—Steve had done enough of that. Also, I knew if there was any chance of getting back on the team I had to bite my tongue, and for the most part, I did. But Steve was still hammering me in the papers at what seemed to be every chance he got. If he had made up his mind, he should have just stated that he was coach and that he had made his final decision. But he never said it and continued to play games in the media.

The article that really put me through the roof was one

that compared me to Eric, since he was on the team and I wasn't, even though we both have strong personalities and we both supposedly disagreed with Steve about where we should play. Steve said that the difference between us was that, "One puts the ball in the back of the net and the other doesn't." Now, I had not been a part of the National Team for 11 years because I was a goal-scorer. The key to my game was, and has always been, my work rate, my ability to play both ways, and my competitive edge. Steve also said that Eric's complaints were more acceptable because he had made them in the press, whereas I had either complained in private or had bad "body language," a comment that totally contradicted Steve's "keep problems within the team" policy. In that same article, Eric stuck his neck out for me again, and I was grateful. Eric's constant support helped get me through. He and his wife, Amy, would call every day just to see how we were doing. I wasn't surprised—Eric has always been a loyal friend. But for him to stand by me when most people were running for cover is something I will never forget. And his support of me didn't make his life any easier in the months to come.

After reading the article, I thought that maybe I was ready to go public. But I knew that would be a mistake, so instead I called Sunil in a rage, and told him that he had better quiet Sampson down. Sunil said he agreed, and that he would speak to Steve. Things seemed to calm down for a little while. No matter what he said, Steve was obviously insecure about his decision to cut me, so he kept trying to justify it in the papers every chance he got. But the issue wouldn't go away because he never offered a legitimate explanation to the press, players, or fans.

The National Team was in town most of the week before the U.S.-Scotland match on May 30. I had the opportunity to talk with Tab, Mike Burns, Alexi, and Eric, and their support of me meant a lot. Scotland was training at D.C. United, so I had a chance to talk to some of them and they offered support, too. Craig Brown, the Scottish manager, passed on his regards as well. The U.S. players said that the last couple of weeks had been unsettling and that there was a lot of discontent. The Federation was moving mountains—relying on a rarely-used immigration loophole—to get David Regis, a French defender, his American citizenship at the last second. It came through right before the Scotland match and players who had fought through qualifying were disgusted, something Steve refused to acknowledge with his "one, big, happy family" comments to the media. Unbelievably, he even made Jeff Agoos room with Regis, the player most likely to move into his spot, and help him study for his citizenship test. Players didn't resent Regis, they resented Steve's inconsistencies and contradictions. One and a half years of traveling to Central America, producing results, and having bags of urine thrown on you by angry fans apparently counted for nothing. The coach who talked about the importance of team chemistry took on players *weeks* before the beginning of the World Cup who had never been on the field with the team. The players also thought it was a slap in the face when Regis was given my old number, six.

By the time the Scotland game rolled around, it was clear to me that I wasn't going to France, but I was still angry about the way it had been handled. If the Federation was interested in having me play for them in the future—as they had mentioned to me—the damage would have to be repaired. The best time to start doing that was before the World Cup, before the results were in. So Craig met with Hank Steinbrecher and Alan Rothenberg the day before the Scotland game to ask for a public apology or at least a positive statement from the Federation about the contributions I had made and would continue to make to soccer in the U.S. They agreed that Steve had handled things badly and said that if the U.S. hadn't won the Austria game, he would've been gone. They also said they would talk to Steve about the apology and Alan promised specifically that the Federation would issue some sort of positive statement. As far as I know, neither the apology nor the supportive statement was ever issued, and we never got an explanation.

Since they were in town, I invited Alexi, Tab, and Eric to

be guests on "Soccer Sweep," the weekly show I co-host with Dave Johnson during the MLS season on NewsChannel 8, a local D.C. cable station. Everything was set to go, until Alexi was suddenly called up to New York for a MetroStars game that weekend. Before the Macedonia game, Alexi had been quoted in the press as saying that players not getting into games with the National Team in May should be allowed to go with their MLS clubs to stay fit. But Sampson adamantly stated in the press that he wanted everyone to be together for the final weeks leading up to France—until the week that Alexi was going to be on my show, that is. He let some other players join their clubs as well, but it was another contradiction. Tab and Eric were still able to come on, but were stopped on their way out of the team hotel and warned by Assistant Coach Clive Charles to watch what they said. My situation with the National Team was considered off-limits.

I had a game for D.C. that weekend in Tampa and watched the Scotland match in my hotel room with Richie Williams. I could see "Where's Johnny" signs in the stands, and Sam's Army had a sign that read "Harkes is Our Captain for Life." It is hard to express how much those signs of support meant to me, along with the thousands of e-mails and letters I received from fans all over the country. Not because they would change anything, but because they kept me going during one of the most difficult periods of my life. As far as the game went, I didn't feel it was the best send-off for the United States.

Once the National Team arrived in France, I received many calls from Chateau Pizay. Ever since Steve dropped me, guys were watching their backs and wondering if they would be the next one to get on his bad side. No one wanted to speak out, and no one trusted each other anymore. Even worse, players were wondering if there was a "rat" among them, someone who had broken the unspoken code of trust that exists among players and gone behind their teammates' backs, betraying confidences, and selling them out for their own benefit. Team unity, forged during Copa America and hardened during qualifying, had melted away.

The new guys had nothing to moan about because they had a trip to France handed to them on a silver platter. Welcome to the National Team: here's a chance to play in the greatest tournament in the world. They didn't have to go through the battles that some of us did. I can't blame them because Steve chose them. But it wasn't fair to them, either. He should have brought them in 18 months earlier and let them work their way onto the team. It's all about consistency, not flash-in-the-pan performances. He was putting a huge amount of pressure on young, internationally inexperienced players like Brian Maissoneuve, telling the press that these guys were critical to the team, when he should have been downplaying their roles to keep them relaxed. He put the most pressure on Claudio, going on about how Claudio would do great things in the World Cup. England coach Glenn Hoddle didn't do that to *Alan Shearer*—how could Steve do that to a 24-year-old player? It was unfair to Claudio and counterproductive. I received calls from players every day the team was in France. Sometimes I felt like I was still part of the team, still captain, because guys would call and tell me their problems. It was more than frustrating though, because I was here and they were there. But they were still my teammates and friends, so I told them to get their heads straight and to remember they were at the World Cup. Enjoy it—go out and perform.

About two days before the first U.S. match, ESPN aired "Outside the Lines," a behind-the-scenes special about the U.S. National Team. ESPN had been trailing us for months during qualifying and we knew what they were working on. But we were never told that Steve would be wearing a microphone while the crew was on the other side of the field. The man who wanted us to settle our difficulties within the team and not in the media was recording us without our knowledge. As I watched the show with Cindi, I felt sick. I had to relive it all over again: the trainings, the injuries, the excitement when we got good results. And the suspense and tension we experienced toward the end of qualifying. But the thing that upset me the most was the locker room shot after we had beaten Canada and finally qualified for the World Cup: Sampson standing there, hugging me, and telling me that I was going to my third World Cup. That hit home. How could he have taken everything away from me? Could I have done things differently? Why had he done this to me? As soon as I saw that scene, I broke down and cried. It was the first time I'd let everything really get to me since I'd been cut.

I watched all of the U.S. World Cup matches at home with Cindi. It was strange to be so far away from a team I had been such a big part of. I didn't really know how to feel: I was angry I wasn't there. I was hopeful that my friends would play well, and when things were going badly, I was frustrated that I couldn't help out. What I really wanted was for Steve to fall flat on his face, but without the team doing the same. But that didn't seem possible.

An hour before the Germany game, Sunil and Tab called me from Parc des Princes in Paris. Both were supportive. It sounded nice, but it didn't change a thing. I wasn't surprised that the U.S. lost 2–0. With the 3-6-1 formation and without strong leadership on the field, we looked like boys against men, 1990 all over again. Eric was the sole attacking player in a defensive system—it looked more like a 3–7—with no distribution into the box, and there wasn't much he could do. Key players who were supposed to rise to the occasion didn't, and were exposed. Germany seemed to take their foot off the gas in the second half. After that match, some of the players started to speak out in the press. Steve was not happy, and in the days following the game, Eric and Alexi were threatened with an early flight home.

The second U.S. match was against Iran, and the team looked good at times. Steve had abandoned the 3-6-1 in favor of a 3-5-2, and dramatically changed the lineup, but that wasn't enough. I couldn't stand to see U.S. soccer lose to a team like Iran—hardly a world soccer power. The U.S. had come so far: from the inexperienced college kids of 1990, to the second round in 1994, to losing to Iran in 1998. They were unlucky with a lot of chances and lost 2–1.

Eric and Lexi called that night at 4:00 A.M. France time

and were miserable. The next day, Brad Friedel, Tab, Eric, Alexi, and Burnsy called me from a tour bus, complaining and saying, "You don't want to be here, Harkesy. It's terrible." Of course I wanted to be there. It killed me that I wasn't there, that I couldn't do anything except watch from 6,000 miles away. Maybe they were trying to be nice, but I could only hear so many complaints. I wished they'd let out these complaints two months earlier.

I was trying to get on with my life and move forward. I was enjoying being with D.C. United and I wanted to focus on that. And, if anything, I was even more aware of what was important to me: I have a wonderful wife, two beautiful, healthy children, a great career, and good friends and family that stick by me through everything. That's what I took away from my experience. I would never want to go through it again, but it reminded me to put things in perspective.

Going into the Yugoslavia match, the boys were playing for pride and nothing else, since the Iran loss ensured the U.S. was not going to the round of 16. The team did OK, but not good enough. They lost 1–0 in an uninspiring match. I was surprised that Steve didn't use players who hadn't played much or at all during the tournament. It would have been a classy thing to do.

The U.S. team finished 32nd out of 32 in the World Cup. Suddenly it was open season on Sampson because his master plan had backfired. I wasn't unhappy to see the harsh comments in the papers, but it was a little late. Late for me, and late for the U.S. The press finally started to criticize Steve, but it was only as the U.S. was packing to go home. Players felt free to say that Steve had ruined things, but their timing was off and they received a lot of criticism after speaking out publicly. Although I agree they should have waited, I thought it was strange that people were so willing to shoot the messengers. These guys had been part of the National Team for years, and had never done or said anything so critical of their coach. Maybe their comments reflected how bad the situation really was. In any case, there were no winners here—not Steve, the players, or U.S. soccer.

218

I can't think of one thing that Steve did right in the months leading up to the World Cup. He seemed to have no respect for or understanding of the tournament. How could he possibly have imagined that he could drop his captain, switch the formation, bring in new players, play people out of position, completely disrupt team chemistry, and still get good results against the best teams in the world playing at the top of their game in the biggest sporting event in the world? To this day, Steve has not accepted any real responsibility for the failure in France, choosing instead to reconstruct history, blame the players, and criticize MLS and the U.S. development system.

Through it all, what Steve failed to recognize was that the veteran players, who had been there since Copa America and throughout qualifying, were the cohesive element of a team that would show up, play, and do the job when it came to big-time games. This core group understood the difference between an important game and a friendly, knew how to pace itself, and was fixated on the World Cup. This may have contributed to our inconsistency, but Steve's failure to recognize it led to his downfall when he dismantled the team just before the World Cup. The veteran players would have been in top form for France and would have played their hearts out, that's for sure.

Ironically, the coaching accomplishments that Steve is so proud of—success at Copa America, beating Brazil, qualifying for France—I was a major part of. That is not to say I was solely responsible for those successes—or that Steve did not contribute in any way—but I did play a big part, both on and off the field. Somewhere along the way, Steve decided he didn't need my leadership anymore, presumably thinking he could manage the team's disparate personalities on his own. But his self-confidence proved to be a big mistake.

When Sampson resigned as coach of the National Team a few days after the U.S. was eliminated, people kept asking me if I felt vindicated.

The answer is no.

There's no vindication because I didn't get to participate

in the World Cup and represent my country. There's no vindication because our team lost, miserably, and now our country has been set back in the world of soccer. And there's no vindication because I lost trust and confidence in people at the Federation who—even if they couldn't override Steve's decision on the merits—could have made sure that his handling of the situation was done with more class and less damage to my reputation.

I'll never know if I would have made a difference at the World Cup, but I do know that things could have been handled a lot differently. The vicious rumors were a disgrace. I know I'm a public figure and that means I'm subject to criticism, but that was unfair to my family. When the team was coming down on Steve after the World Cup, he called players, asking them to take it easy on him because he was a "human being," something he didn't seem to remember when he was dealing with me.

But even if it is too late for the '98 team, it's not too late for U.S. soccer. Everyone who cares about the development of soccer in this country needs to think about where they want it to go, how they want it to develop. We suffered a setback and that's when people start to ask questions. But we can't dwell on the past. U.S. soccer needs to move forward and think about where it's going.

If anything should be learned here, it's that we are in desperate need of coaches with experience. The fiasco that took place during the 1998 World Cup should be expected when someone who has never played or coached professionally is allowed to manage the National Team. It's hard as a player to respect a coach who doesn't have the same knowledge or experience that you do. It's like a lawyer working for a paralegal and the paralegal keeps telling the lawyer how to do his job. We need coaches who have experienced the game at the highest level and understand the commitment and discipline that's necessary to succeed there. We need coaches who can handle different personalities. We need coaches who can spot a young, talented player, take him aside, and help him develop his game.

It's not about winning the World Cup in 2010, although that would be fantastic. It's important to remember that, in 1998, France became only the seventh country in the history of the World Cup to win the title. A country doesn't decide or presume to decide when it's going to win the World Cup. But we do need to focus on creating a system that identifies, develops, and brings together a broad spectrum of young talent—talent that will be ready to make their mark by 2010, or sooner. Professional players—especially the core group of veteran players on the current National Team—have to be involved, and I plan on being one of them. I want to be involved at any level: on the field or off, with a team or with the Federation. I would love to work with the under-17s, under-20s, National Team, or other youth teams. I would consider it an honor. I want our teenagers to compete against the best in the world so that clubs in England are fighting to steal our 18-year-olds away from MLS. But we can't have shortcuts. We have to have a system in place that will work over a long period of time.

Soccer is experiencing some growing pains right now, and that means we have to be patient. That also means we have to hire the right people. We need people who have it in their heart to do what's good for soccer, not just for themselves and for the bottom line. We need people who believe in the sport and what they can do for it. We don't need people who look at soccer as something they own or as just another business venture that's there to be taken advantage of until something else comes along. MLS investors, in particular, must be patient.

I'm a soccer player and I've never pretended to be anything else. My life took a bizarre twist in 1998 and it wasn't one that I wanted, expected, or would wish on anyone else. But it's not over for me—far from it. I'm fortunate enough to play this game and I love it. I've never given up, and I've worked nonstop at the only career I ever wanted.

And for anyone else who wants to become a professional soccer player, I hope that they do the same thing and that we have a system in place that will bring the best out of them.

Playing with 1996–97 MLS Cup Champions, D.C. United.

Despite everything that might happen along the way, I hope they're persistent and stick with it.

Because it's all been worth it to me. And no matter what you accomplish, there are always new challenges and something more to prove.

222

Epilogue

A new year brings possibility, opportunity, and things you'll never expect. I would never have predicted the twists and turns that my career took in 1998, that's for sure. Looking back, I'm tempted to think, "Thank *God* 1998 is behind me." On the other hand, I am thankful that after such a negative experience with the National Team, I was able to channel my energies into something positive with D.C. United. Oddly enough, although D.C. United didn't bring home the MLS Cup for the third year in a row, it was the club's best season yet.

D.C. United produced great results on the field and won unprecedented international respect and exposure for itself and MLS. As a start, we won the CONCACAF Champions' Cup in August, beating Mexican champions Toluca, 1–0, in the final. The CONCACAF Cup has always been dominated by Mexican clubs, and it was a major test of what MLS and D.C. have to offer international soccer. We played exceptionally well throughout the tournament and were crowned champions of North America, Central America, and the Caribbean—the first U.S. club to win the tournament since it began in 1962. Just as important, by winning, D.C. United qualified as the CONCACAF representative for the Inter-American Cup, a "home-and-away" championship between the two best clubs in North and South America.

Although things were going well for the team on the field, the future seemed a little unsettled because of ongoing speculation about whether Bruce would be named the new National Team coach. Everyone was curious about who would be chosen to pick up the pieces after the World Cup—foreign or American coach?—and in what direction the new coach would go—youth vs. veterans, etc. There was early talk of Bora coming back or Carlos Quieroz moving into the spot. Bruce appeared to be the leading candidate, but no one knew if he would get it, and if he did, when he would start. The process stalled in mid-August after Alan Rothenberg's term as President of the Federation expired and new President, Robert Contiguglia, took office promising to take a fresh look at the candidates.

The MLS playoffs began in late September and our attitude going in was different from other years. We fully expected to make it back to the final, but felt a little more pressure to win our third in a row—to "threepeat." We started off against the Miami Fusion—an expansion team with something to prove—and we were glad to finish them off in two. Our best-of-three playoff series against the Columbus Crew for the Eastern Conference title was tough—three games in eight days with game two on that tight field of theirs in the rain.

The expansion Chicago Fire took care of the Los Angeles Galaxy early in the Western Conference, beating the Galaxy in an unexpected two-game sweep, and got an eight-day rest before playing us in MLS Cup '98 at the Rose Bowl in Pasadena. Even though D.C. had only three days to get ready for the final, we were still heavily favored to win.

The game itself felt a little off, and the fatigue showed in our play. After playing the last MLS final at home in RFK, the difference in atmosphere was noticeable. Going into the game, we were ready to play, but the Fire seemed hungrier and we ended up losing 2–0. Our rhythm was off, we missed a few early chances, and a few calls went against us, things that can change the outcome of a game. Full credit is due the Chicago players and first-year coach Bob Bradley, Bruce's former assistant at D.C. United. Although I still believe D.C. was the better team, on that day, *they* won, deservedly so.

After the MLS Cup, D.C. got a little break before preparing for our toughest challenge yet—facing Brazilian powerhouse Vasco da Gama in the InterAmerican Cup. Just days after the final, Bruce was named National Team coach, which meant the Vasco matches would be his last with United. Former New England coach Thomas Rongen and former National Team coach Bob Gansler were the leading candidates to take his place at the club.

The first Vasco game was at RFK, which was great not just because it gave us home-field advantage, but because it allowed me to spend more time at home with Cindi, who had her second reconstructive knee surgery just four days before the game. The game drew the biggest crowd of the season at RFK—over 26,000 fans—and the atmosphere was ideal. We went after Vasco right from the start, really pressured them, and had a number of good scoring chances. Unfortunately, we gave up a goal early in the second half and lost 1–0. We felt good about the way we'd played and knew going down to Florida for the second game that we were still in it, although we would have to win by at least two goals under the tiebreaker system.

Just before we left for the game, Thomas Rongen was announced as the next head coach of D.C., and he traveled with us so he could get a look at his new team. It was ironic to me that Thomas would now be my coach after he had been so interested in getting me to New England a year earlier. Although things had not gone Thomas' way with the Revolution, he had been very successful in Tampa Bay, and the National Team players on D.C. were familiar with him from his time as an assistant coach for Steve Sampson.

Game two against Vasco was even better than game one. Unfortunately the crowd was disappointing. Only 7,000 fans turned out at Lockhart Stadium for one of the biggest games ever for a U.S. club team. But we were still excited to be on that field, and in the end, we played the better soccer and won 2–0. There was talk in the media about how tired Vasco was after traveling four days earlier from Japan after a 2–1 loss to Real Madrid in the Toyota Cup, the world club championship. But tired or not, there was no way that a squad like Vasco wanted to lose to us—an *American* club team—and they came at us with all they had. In fact, they had even more at stake after losing to Real Madrid since they did not want to return to Brazil empty-handed. They made only one change to the lineup that played in the Toyota Cup, which showed they took us seriously. We took control of the game early on and put some dangerous balls into the box, which helped boost our confidence. A goal from Tony Sanneh in the 34th minute gave us the lead and a goal from Eddie Pope late in the second half gave us the championship.

The win was huge, but unfortunately the majority of the press coverage was in Brazil. That was a real shame, although it is hard to complain when only a few thousand people show up. Still, we had earned the most important win in MLS' three-year history and were crowned champions of the Western Hemisphere. Back in 1996, no one would have expected such success from an MLS club in so short a time. And we were at the end of a very long season. From training in January through our last game in December, we had played close to 11 months of soccer.

I'm proud of what we've built at D.C. United. It is a strong club on and off the field and has developed a chemistry that is hard to find in clubs that have been around for a while, let alone three years. D.C. United is easily the league's most valuable and credible asset. It would be foolish and short-sighted for MLS to break up the team because of salary cap concerns, as is rumored.

It's impossible to know what the coming year holds. Bruce and I have had discussions about my role on the National Team. He has seen me play for over 15 years and knows what I can do. I would certainly be happy to play for him at yet another level. But with the 2002 World Cup four years away, it is the ideal time for him to look at new faces. Bruce knows that one of the keys to success at the National Team level is to blend youth with experience.

As for the future of professional soccer in this country, MLS needs to continue to progress, both on and off the field. Hopefully, the league will be persuaded to build more soccer-only facilities, which will not only provide a better atmosphere for games, but improve the league's finances by eliminating the exorbitant rent that many clubs currently pay and creating new revenue streams in the form of parking, concessions, and luxury boxes. Only time will tell how things work out. For now, it is critically important for fans to take on more responsibility for the success of the league by being supportive and showing up at stadiums.

As for my future in MLS, I would love to stay with United. Who wouldn't given its success. But if I've learned anything, it's that you can't tell how things will work out. It would be strange to move, but if that happens, it happens. No matter where I am, I want to look back on my years in MLS knowing I put everything into pushing the game to the highest level. I truly believe that someday we will be there.

Photo Credits

All photographs supplied by John Harkes, except those noted below: